Candle
Magic

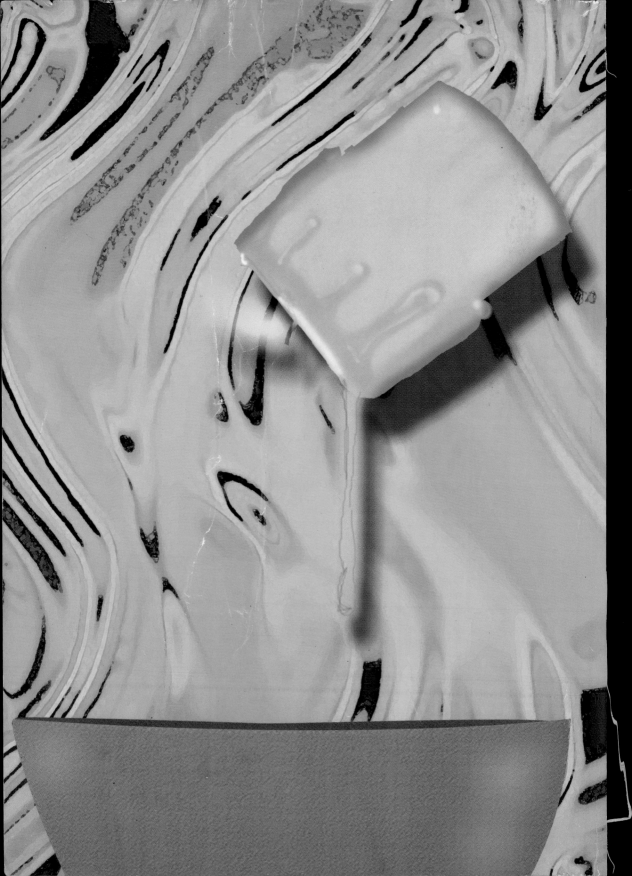

The Ultimate Full-color Guide

Candle Magic

Batia Shorek

Astrolog Publishing House Ltd.

Editor: Judy Bar-on
Cover Design: Na'ama Yaffe
Language Consultant: Judy Bar-on
Layout and Graphics: Daniel Akerman
Production Manager: Dan Gold

P.O. Box 1123, Hod Hasharon 45111, Israel
Tel: 972-9-7412044
Fax: 972-9-7442714
E-Mail: info@astrolog.co.il
Astrolog Web Site: www.astrolog.co.il

ISBN 965-494-147-3

Published by Astrolog Publishing House 2003

10 9 8 7 6 5 4 3 2 1

Index

Index

Fire and humankind

Who among us does not have at least one fond memory of a time when fire was an integral part of a "magical" event? The memory may be as prosaic as candles on a birthday cake, or as catastrophic as a raging forest fire. We may have lounged around a campfire, staring endlessly into the glowing embers, or even meditated on the coals after preparing steaks on the backyard grill. The family hearth, although not commonly used in Western society for food preparation, is nonetheless a central gathering place in many homes. The flames, the coals, the shapes and patterns created by the dancing fire and the embers, are a source of infinite fascination and comfort to just about everyone.

Humankind has a dichotomous relationship with the element. While fire commands a deep respect and fear, it is also a friendly and useful commodity. Fire's capacity to destroy and devastate goes hand in hand with its flexibility and adaptability to man's whims and desires. Fire can be created and controlled under certain circumstances. But just as we can adapt fire to our needs, we never lose sight of the fact that fire has a life of its own, and is ultimately a force beyond our control and understanding.

And so over the span of history, fire has featured in a wide range of human activities, both sacred and profane. Fire has been called into service in virtually every area of human life. It is in the realm of the sacred that we see the development of the use of fire for magic.

Early cultures regarded fire as so precious and vital that it was assumed to have been granted by generous and powerful gods. In Greek mythology, we meet the god of fire, Hephaestus. Prometheus steals fire from Hephaestus for use by mortals, which is forbidden by Zeus, the king of the gods. Indian and Maori legends also include gods who provide fire for the people. The sun was also worshipped, and in some traditions the sun-god and the fire-god were one and the same. Some cultures even worshipped the sun itself as a deity.

Whoever among mortal men was the keeper of the fire was considered to have a sacred mission, and fire was guarded jealously.

Today, religious ritual in virtually every tradition includes fire. Catholics and Jews burn so-called eternal lights in their churches and synagogues. Catholic churches also use votive candles to accompany the prayers offered by the faithful to the saints or the Virgin. Many religions use candles in a variety of ceremonies. Every holy day on the Jewish calendar is marked by the lighting of candles at sundown. Hanukkah, the festival of lights, celebrates the miracle of a flame that kept burning long after its fuel should have run out. Jews also burn memorial candles to mark the anniversary of a loved one's passing.

Modern Christmas trees are lit with electric lights, but this tradition originated from trees decked with candles.

Something about a flame, however tiny, brings out a primal spiritual connection in the people who behold it. The flame sets the stage for rituals to be even more powerful and magical for the participants.

Man's desire to make fire portable and easily controlled when used indoors led to the invention of candles hundreds of years before the Common Era. While there is no record of the invention of the very first candle, we do know of early candle use. Archeological artifacts such as candle holders have been found dating back to the fourth century BCE.

In the New World, candles were used in the first century CE by Native Americans who burned oily fish wedged into wood. In the upper northeast of America, early settlers made wax from berries, which they fashioned into candles resembling those we use today.

Tallow, which is made by melting the fat of animals, pouring the fat into molds, and cooling it, was widely used as an early candle material. Tallow was inexpensive, but had an offensive odor. Those who could afford it preferred beeswax candles or oil lamps.

In Europe, around the 1500s, the use of molds for candle-making became widely accepted. Additives were discovered that could improve the consistency of the wax, making molded candles more stable and decorative. In the 19th century, candle-making machines were invented and candles of a much higher quality than was previously possible were produced. These manufactured candles were mostly made of paraffin, which was developed during the same century. When stearin was added to paraffin candles in the latter part of the 1800s, the result was very similar to modern candles. Tallow candles all but disappeared from use with the advent of paraffin.

Candles are often used at prayer vigils, at ceremonial occasions of all kinds, and even at political demonstrations. They are used to set the mood at parties and various types of gatherings. It is as if we intuitively understand that the ritual of lighting the candle, the energy of the flame, and the way these change the energy of the immediate environment, are magical. Candles can foster feelings of serenity, of calm, and of sanctity.

When candles are used for religious ritual or celebration, they cause a shift in the vibrations of the people and environment from profane to sacred.

Even when a candle is lit in a room in a home, that home is somehow transformed, exuding a feeling of sanctity or simply a special atmosphere. This shift in energy is perceptible, and can be used to perform magic.

Paradise   Hieronymus Bosch   Hell

Magic

"Magic" in the modern vernacular most often refers to "sleight of hand" or to a show by a magician who practices illusion. We have been conditioned to believe that real magic does not exist, and that the magician is a trickster, combining skill and practice to provide us with a performance that perplexes and delights us.

We may also use the word "magic" to describe that which we simply don't understand. "Maybe it was magic!" is usually uttered with tongue in cheek. Or we might say, "It was simply magical!" and mean it was awe-inspiring, and elicited strong emotion.

And yet, true magic is possible. When we accept the existence of an energy that is unseen and ubiquitous, and in fact constitutes ourselves and everything that exists, we allow for other beliefs to surface and make it possible for us to embrace the improbable, the illogical, the inexplicable... and the magical.

We can use the awesome power of our thoughts and feelings to influence that energy. Thus we can become connected to everything that exists, and perform true miracles. When we accept that our thoughts precede our reality, and that everything we do and everything we are we first created in our thoughts, we then see that each of us has the ability to be a "magician." Through magic we can gain more control over our world and our destiny.

Many of our familiar rituals are actually the performance of magic. We may light the birthday candles thinking that it is simply a time-honored tradition that is fun for children. But what is the child actually doing? Candle magic. He conjures a vision of his desire, looks at the flame and utters his wish in his mind, and then extinguishes the flame, believing his wish will come true. He uses his mind to create a reality, and uses the energy of the candles to consecrate his ritual.

Magic is the affecting of events using the power of our mind and feelings.

We must accept that our mind and feelings have power before we can proceed to performing magic. We must suspend our need to understand events according to logic and science. We must embrace our ability to manifest results. The fact is, we are affecting our lives through our thoughts every moment of our existence! Once we consciously harness that power, we can effect dramatic changes in every aspect.

The candle ritual you perform, together with the focused concentration of attention and

intention, will cause a magical outcome. The magic itself is actually setting the energy in motion to make your goal come about in the physical world. Alone, the candle's flame and the words you choose cannot perform magic, but when combined with the powerful energy of your focused intention – the power of your mind – a spell is cast and the magic is set in motion.

The magic we perform with candles may not bring instantaneous results every time, although there are incidences where the effect is immediate and dramatic. Some magic has to be patiently nurtured. But the energies will shift each time we perform a magic ritual, and results will occur. Some magic rituals need to be performed repeatedly until a result is noticed, since energy needs to be built up toward some more difficult goals. Candle magic can be a very powerful medium to manifest your desires, but it cannot be rushed or pushed. Magic performed for healing or success in love may take a buildup of magic energy before progress can be detected, for example. Don't give up if you don't see the desired results immediately. Keep your intention strong and persevere with your candle magic ritual.

When asking for a specific outcome, always add, "Or something better." This makes you aware that your specific wish may not be appropriate, but that you are open to "something better" that the universe can conjure up for you, if it is not the right time or circumstance for you to receive what you believe you desire.

Keep in mind that some magic, after it has worked and brought about the desired result, may need to be repeated in order to keep the energy working in that direction. In other words, the magic you've put into motion can "wear out" and may need periodic replenishing.

Elements of candle magic

Candle magic is easy to learn and perform. It requires only basic and easily available materials as well as simple rituals. The basic elements we need are:

1. An altar or other suitable place to perform magic;

2. Candles and candle paraphernalia (holders, matches, lighters, snuffers, etc.);

3. Helping substances: oils, herbs, incense;

4. Magic spells.

Candle magic can be pressed into service for many goals. The possibilities are as limitless as your imagination. Here are but a few examples of goals you may have for your candle magic:

1. Manifestation of change. Perhaps you would like to change some aspect of your usual behavior or outlook on life. You might want to become more outgoing or increase your self-esteem. You may wish to move to a new location, find a new job, or even change career direction.

2. Help in a relationship. You might use your magic to help you strengthen an existing relationship, find a new mate or life partner, or gain insights into your relationship with a parent, child, or friend.

3. Money and abundance. Candle magic can be used to focus on bringing more wealth and financial stability into your life. Repayment of debts owing to you and acquiring enough money to pay the bills are common goals.

There is no reason that magic cannot be utilized to attain material goals. There is nothing "unspiritual" about wanting abundance or riches.

4. **Success and career.** You may be stagnating in your job or feeling as if success in your career is eluding you. If you are starting a new venture, you may want to use the magic to concentrate energies for its success.

5. **Release of undesirable elements.** Candle magic can serve to help break unwanted habits, to repel undesirable energies that may be aimed at us, or to release unwanted emotions or physical symptoms.

6. **Consecration.** A new home or office, a new job, a new baby, or after recovering from an illness are good times to consecrate our space and dedicate it to the energy we wish to perpetuate in it. Candle rituals can be powerful in this regard.

7. **Healing.** Physical, psychological, and mental healing can all be effected through the use of candle magic. Health can be fortified and maintained, or disease can be banished from the body by concentrating thought, belief and energy in a healing ritual.

8. **Decision-making.** Our conscious minds sometimes make it difficult for us to choose between two or more alternatives. Candle magic can put us in touch with our true desires and help in decision-making.

9. **Divination.** Divination is the foretelling of the future. It is asking questions and receiving answers. It is perhaps the most fascinating and popular use of magic.

Never use candle magic to cause harm to another person, or to attempt to manipulate their actions or emotions.

The altar

It is a good idea to have a designated place for your candle magic that is not in a busy area of your home. Choose a place where the candles can burn undisturbed, and where you will not be interrupted when performing magic rituals. Some people select a place in the home where they prepare a permanent altar that they use for magic and for displaying sacred items. This altar can then be used for meditation, which in turn will strengthen its ability to carry out magic for the person whose energies it has absorbed. An altar can be set up in any room of the house where it is likely to be undisturbed.

The altar can be a small table or shelf, or even a box. If the altar is of a flammable material, you can cover it with aluminum foil or a metal tray. Be sure the surface is clean and clear of any unwanted energies. The altar should never be used for any other purpose or by anyone other than the person performing the magic, and should be esthetically pleasing.

If you share a room, or there is no appropriate place in your home for a permanent altar, it is a good idea to dedicate an "altar cloth." This can be any small, decorative tablecloth that you purchase or keep especially for your magic, and that is special and esthetically pleasing to you. Each time you perform candle magic, before you begin your ritual, you can spread your altar cloth in the temporary place you have chosen, thus creating a portable altar. This cloth should be stored in a special place and used only for magic. Your altar candles and other objects should be stored with the cloth and used only for magic. Like the candles themselves, your altar decorations and tools should not be used in other ways in the home.

Decorate your altar with objects that are meaningful to you. If there is a deity you feel attuned to, place a small statue of him or her on your altar. Flowers, crystals or other objects can strengthen the energies around your altar. Place at least one permanent altar candle toward the back of the surface. This will anchor the energies and help to consecrate the altar for its purpose. Some people believe you should have one black and one white candle as your altar candles, but this depends on your preference. If you prefer, you can use just a single altar candle. In this case, it should be white. Altar candles should not burn all the way down during each ritual, as should the candles used for the magic. They can be long-lasting pillar or glass-encased candles that can be reused for several or many magic rituals. Place a decorative incense holder near the altar candles.

Be sure you have a supply of candle-holders on hand as well as a lighter. Candles used for magic should never be lit with a sulfur match. In fact, a supply of simple white candles, which can be lit with the lighter and thereafter used to light the other candles, is ideal.

For some magic, you will extinguish the candle before it has burned itself out. Your altar should be equipped with a candle-snuffer for this purpose. Blowing out the candle will interfere with the energy of the magic. You may want to wet your fingers and "pinch" out the flame, but a snuffer is most convenient.

It might be a good idea to keep slips of paper, a writing utensil, and a small knife or pin near the altar for inscribing wishes that will be used in the magic. The pin can be used to mark the candles with letters and other symbols, and the paper and pencil for writing wishes or inscriptions that will be burned as part of the magic. A metal or earthenware bowl for this purpose should also be kept nearby.

Be absolutely certain that your altar is not located near any flammable object or source of air current such as an open window or air-conditioning vent. Keep your altar clean and organized even when you are not performing magic. When spending time in the presence of your altar, try to maintain a relaxed state of mind, and the altar and its artifacts will attune to you, making your magic all the more powerful.

Candles

Candles can be obtained in a dizzying array of sizes, shapes, colors, and containers. The choices are almost infinite, and in the past several years have mushroomed as candles become ever more popular. In most communities, there is at least one entire store that is devoted to candles and their accessories. Take your time browsing among as large a selection as you can find. Let your intuition guide you toward the right candles for you. Get to know the types of candles available and sense their qualities by holding and touching them. Scent, however should be used very carefully, if at all. Non-scented candles are actually best for magic.

Color, which we will discuss at length, has great power and significance in magic, and the choice of the right color candle for each magic goal is vital.

Figure candles have been molded into human or animal or other types of forms. A figure candle can be used for magic to increase the energy surrounding a particular goal. For instance, a candle in the form of embracing lovers can be used when asking for passion to come into your life, or to attract more passion into your relationship. Candles depicting deities can also be used. Each deity symbolizes a particular human characteristic or type of luck or experience.

Double- and triple-action candles incorporate two or three colors into a single candle. A half-black and half-white candle, for instance, might be chosen for a ritual in which you want the powers of good to supercede those of evil. A red, white, and green candle might be burned for blessing and good luck.

Choose according to what feels right for the magic you want to manifest. As a rule, it is best not to choose elaborately shaped candles that are not esthetic, depict frivolous items, or are overly thick or large. Avoid candles that contain substances such as glitter or have been decorated with stickers, dried flowers, paper, and other added materials. These will cause the candle to burn unevenly, and can interrupt your concentration. The candle may smoke or sputter, and the results of the magic will be compromised.

Glass-encased candles can be cleaner to use, and safer when leaving a candle burning unattended for a period of time. They are also useful for magic rituals that entail burning over a period of several days. You might be able to find seven-day candles or multi-layer candles encased in glass for use in magic rituals that need to be repeated over several days, or for use as permanent altar candles. Seven-knob/pointed candles that are not glass-encased are also useful for longer rituals. Pillar candles can be purchased with varying thickness and height, and can also be quite long-lasting, although they often change shape as they are burned over time, and need to be carefully supervised.

Traditional six-inch straight candles or votives are probably the easiest to use for candle magic. They burn down within a few hours, and come in a large variety of colors. Votive candles can be of the type that melts into a puddle of wax, or they can be of the non-drip type. Either can be used, according to the magic being performed and the need for wax formations, which will be discussed later on.

If handmade candles are chosen, they should be used with care. The candle-maker will have infused the candle with his or her own energies, which can affect the magic, unless the candle is purified before use. Even candles that have been mass produced will have absorbed energy from people who previously handled them, and they will contain those vibrations until purified. In order to check your candle for purity of vibration, hold a crystal pendulum over the candle. If the pendulum swings freely forward and backward or in a clockwise direction, the candle is vibrating positively and can be used. If the pendulum swings side to side or counterclockwise, however, this means that the candle is vibrating negatively and should be purified before use. Rinse the candle in pure mineral or distilled water, and pass it through the smoke of incense made of sage or frankincense. You should now be able to perform the pendulum test with a positive result.

Taking the time to make your own candles for your magic can prove to be a very satisfying activity and add strength to your magic. You can be creative, and at the same time infuse your candles with your own vibrations, synchronizing them with your energies, and intensifying their efficacy as conduits for magic.

Entire books on the art of candle-making are available, and there is no end to the variety of candles you can produce. We will discuss this here so far as it pertains to candles that you make specifically for use in magic.

Start with your magic goal in mind, and decide what color or colors you will be using before you shop for your candle-making materials. You will most likely want to use paraffin wax, although there are other choices. Paraffin usually provides a good quality, slow-burning candle. The wick should be braided and should not have a metal core, as the metal can be released into the air when burned and have adverse health affects. The size of the wick will vary according to candle size. Square braids usually burn most evenly.

Candle dyes come in a large variety of colors, and since they can be mixed, you can make a candle of virtually any color you desire. A very important advantage of making your own candles is your ability to adjust the color to exactly the color frequency that resonates with you. If you take your time when formulating the color and choose and mix while thinking about your magic, you will produce a candle that is just the right color for you and your magic.

It is preferable not to use scent or oils when making candles for magic. Scent can certainly enhance your magic, but is best introduced in the form of incense or oil that is used to dress or anoint the candle. This will be discussed at length later on. It is also not advisable to decorate your candles with flowers or other decorative substances as this can cause the candle to burn unevenly and jeopardize the magic result.

Other additives, such as certain types of crystal substances can be added at your discretion. Consult with the assistant at the store where you purchase your materials, and keep in mind your magic purpose when deciding whether to add a substance that might prolong or shorten the burning time of your candle, or otherwise change its consistency.

Stearic acid, which is commonly added to candles, can make the color appear lighter, more pastel, and will cause the candle to burn more slowly and evenly.

Choose the molds you will use for your candle-making according to the purpose of the magic and your goal. Many commercial molds in all shapes and sizes imaginable are available. Be careful not to choose molds that are too large or too elaborately and unevenly shaped. Many disposable items you have at home will do nicely for candle molds. By using a large empty jam jar, you can produce a glass-encased candle that you might want to leave burning for several days, if this is appropriate to your magic. Earthenware flower-pots can work as well for this purpose. Smaller jars, such as small baby-food jars, can be filled from half-full to completely full, making wonderful smaller candles for magic. Frozen juice cans also come in various sizes and make excellent molds.

While making your candles, try to work alone, in a serene atmosphere where you will not be disturbed or interrupted. Try to maintain a meditative mood and concentrate on your magic goal while making your candles. This will infuse your candles with extra power to work for you in your magic. When your candles are ready, try to begin your magic ritual soon afterward. If you need to store your homemade candles until you perform your magic, keep them in a place where they will be undisturbed.

Astrological candles are used to symbolize the person performing the magic, or another person involved in the goal of your magic. You can purchase or make a candle with your astrological sign or which represents your sign in some other way (such as color), or you can inscribe your sign on the candle with a small blade, pin, or nail.

Candles can be simple or elaborately decorated and shaped, according to your wish. Try to choose candles that feel right to you, and keep your declared desire firmly in mind when choosing. Use your intuition and the candle will "tell" you that it is the right one for your particular goal.

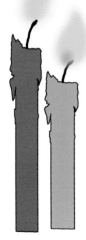

The size of your candle should be taken into consideration. If you want your candles to burn down completely, and you have only a few hours, try to use short votive candles, small, thin tapers, small straight candles, or even tea lights. Tea lights are small round candles usually no more than 3/4 inch in height, and encased in a metal jacket. They are versatile and safe, and will burn completely within a few hours.

Candle magic should always be performed using new and as yet unlit candles. Candles that have already been partly burned are not appropriate.

Even candles that have been used, unlit, as decoration in the home are not fit for magic. They have absorbed vibrations from the events in the environment and cannot be considered fresh or virgin. Always use new candles bought or made for the purpose of candle magic.

When you bring your candles home, be sure to clean them thoroughly with a cloth, or even with a mild cleaning solution. Be careful when storing candles to keep them separate from one another so that they do not receive nicks, and keep them free of dust. When storing several candles together, wrapping each individually in a small plastic bag can keep them clean and in good condition. Store candles away from light to prevent their dyes from fading and preserve the integrity of their colors. It is advisable to trim the wicks of the candles to a uniform length before beginning a ritual.

Candle-holders and containers come in a huge variety of sizes, shapes, and materials. Be sure the candle-holders you choose are sturdy and safe. Each candle should stand in its own separate holder, as opposed to candelabras and such. The holders do not have to be decorative or elaborate. Any safe container or surface will suffice.

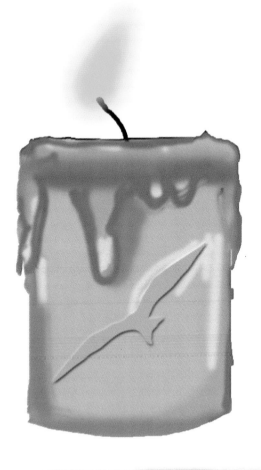

Candle colors

The color you choose for your magic is highly significant and can impact the outcome of your magic considerably. For each color, there are specific energies that can strengthen your ritual, as long as you choose the appropriate color for what you want to manifest.

Each color of the spectrum vibrates at a different frequency. These vibrations affect us in profound ways, even when we are unconscious of their effects. The colors of our environment, the colors in nature, the colors we choose to wear, all have meaning, and change our own frequency of vibration when we are in their presence. Do not underestimate the power of color on candle magic. However, be sure to take into consideration your own particular affinity or feelings for a particular color. You may have attributed meaning and significance to certain colors as a result of your own experiences with them in the past. Ultimately, it is your personal energies that are most important, and if you intuitively feel that a certain color is right (or wrong) for your magic, go with your feelings.

Below is a guide to help you choose the right color for each magic ritual you undertake. Each color symbolizes and vibrates with particular attributes.

White

Spirituality, peace, truth, purity and purification (space clearing), meditation, imagination, inspiration, wholeness. Sometimes associated with death and mourning, or new beginnings. Especially useful for divination.

White can be chosen for any magic and infused with the vibrations of your intentions. It is the only balanced color, while at the same time containing the attributes above. White can be substituted for any other color candle when you can't find the color you need.

Silver

Psychic power, meditation, connection to other dimensions, clairvoyance, memory of past lives. Encourages stability.

Gold

Fast luck, money, good fortune, financial success, justice, career, intuition, protection. Also fosters knowledge and healing, and attracts cosmic influence.

Black

Deep meditation, banishing evil forces, deep levels of consciousness, reversing something, removing negative influence, protection from evil, removing blockages. The black energy is very powerful and should be used with care, lest you suffer from its energy coming back to you in undesirable ways. Never use black for selfish purposes or to inflict harm, since this will only affect your energies for the worse.

Red

Passion, physical strength, desire, and sexual potency. Fosters will power, courage, drive and ambition. Use to overcome fear or inaction.

Brown

Grounding, centering and balance – connection with nature and the earth. Use for attracting money and for diverting financial crisis. Facilitates intuition, concentration, and study. Good for organization of the household. Use for finding lost objects and telepathy.

Grey

Neutral color. Can neutralize or cancel negative energies. Stability.

Pink

Purest and truest love. Friendship and affection, service, and love between family members. Can be used for nurturing romance and respect in relationships and for fighting depression. Enhances reconciliation efforts. The color of femininity.

Magenta

A powerful color that is a combination of red and purple, magenta vibrates at a powerful frequency that promotes rapid change and spiritual healing.

Burned with other colors, it can facilitate speedier magical action.

Orange

Organization, concentration. Good for resolving legal situations. Helps with job success, dealing with change and independence. Fosters creativity, enthusiasm, and mental reasoning. Orange is a powerful force for change.

Yellow

The color of happiness, optimism, and inspiration. Yellow can aid the intellect and the memory, and support creativity. It fosters mental clarity and confidence, as well as energetic activity and good communication. Can strengthen powers of persuasion. Good for moving or relocating.

Purple

Purple vibrates success and protection. Use for luck in business and for progress with projects. Attracts honor, respect, and business contacts, and can eliminate bad luck. Purple is also associated with psychic ability, contact with the spirit world, divination, and meditation.

Royal blue

Happiness, expansiveness, laughter, peace. A powerful color that can foster loyalty and success and harmony within a group. The color of truth and higher guidance. Use for success in exams or for good luck when traveling. Good for curing diseases or recovering from injuries.

Light blue

For inner peace, protection, understanding, patience, and tranquility. Fosters fidelity and harmony in the home.

Indigo (dark purplish blue)

Good for meditation. Halts another person's actions or competition. Balances karma, deters gossip.

Green

Green is the color of growth and fertility, and of abundance. Use for gaining material abundance and wealth. Associated with renewal and fresh starts, such as birth or a new job. Use also for fostering healing and good health and for the health of children.

Candle colors and astrological signs.

Each of the signs of the Zodiac corresponds to one or more colors. When using a candle to represent your sign, choose the color for which you feel the greatest affinity.

Aries — (March 21 to April 20) – red, white;

Taurus — (April 21 to May 21) – green, pink, red, blue;

Gemini — (May 22 to June 21) – yellow, silver, green, red, blue;

Cancer — (June 22-July 22) – metallic blue, silver;

Leo — (July 23 to August 23) – orange, gold, red, green;

Virgo — (August 24 to September 23) – yellow, gold, black, gray;

Libra — (September 24 to October 23) – blue, pink, black;

Scorpio — (October 24 to November 22) – red, silvery gray, black, brown;

Sagittarius — (November 23-December 21) – purple, royal blue, gold, red;

Capricorn — (December 22 to January 20) – black, dark brown, red;

Aquarius — (January 21 to February 19) – light and dark blue, green;

Pisces — (February 20 to March 20) – aquamarine, green, royal blue, white.

Helping substances

Your magic can be intensified by introducing certain other articles and substances that can help. Magic can certainly be performed using only candles, but by introducing these helpers, you multiply the energies and increase your success. Crystals, natural oils, incense and herbs all have properties that can greatly enhance your magic.

Crystals

We are familiar with semi-precious gems and crystals as objects of beauty and as jewelry or ornaments. However, their use and appeal throughout history have been much broader than most people are aware. Crystals have long been used in connection with healing and protection. Evidence of crystal use and belief in their powers exists from biblical times and locations, as well from ancient America and the Far East. Crystals were considered sacred and magical gifts from God that were highly valued, traded, and treasured. Power amulets made from crystals were worn by warriors, and rulers wore charms and jewels not just for beauty, but for spiritual protection and power as well.

The addition of crystals to your candle magic will intensify and magnify the power of your ritual or spell. Not only will they work together with the candle to increase its power, they will also enhance your mental and psychic energies and concentrate them more forcefully.

Crystals abound in a vast variety of densities, colors, and textures. And within these, there is more variety in subtle molecular make-up. Each crystal possesses unique powers and characteristics, which makes choosing the right crystal for your magic essential. Crystals can be purchased at rock stores, which specialize in rocks for collectors, or at various New Age stores where the assistants may be able to help you choose your crystals according to their energetic properties.

To begin with, you might choose a crystal in a color similar to that of the candle you have chosen for your magic. When you have become familiar with the powers of the various crystals, you can refine your choices. But choose carefully, so that the crystal energies will enhance your magic, and not conflict with it.

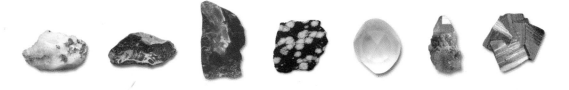

Your crystal does not have to be large, polished or fancy to be effective.

In fact, often the tiniest stones can emit powerful energy adequately and enhance your magic significantly. When deciding which crystal to choose, take your time. Approach the crystals that look attractive to you, and then refine your choice by using your intuition. Try to be with the crystal for a few moments, and feel its effect on you. Do you feel an affinity for it? Close your eyes. Each crystal gives off an energy field that you can detect by running your hands over the crystal, touching it, and holding it.

Choose the crystal that seems to choose you! Regardless of its visual attractiveness, the crystal you are drawn to is the right one for you.

Use crystals that you are attracted to strongly and feel comfortable with. They will work best for your magic.

As with your candles, the color of your crystals will tell you something about its vibration and the type of magic it will be most useful for. Here is a general but by no means exhaustive list of crystal properties by color and name.

White crystals

Apophyllite, selenite, snowy quartz, white opal

The white crystals facilitate connection with our spiritual guides, serenity, and clarity of mind.

Apophyllite promotes balance and aids in divination and communication with other realms.

White opal Enhances visualization and brings out creativity and passion. Said to treat physical ills such as infections and fevers, and to regulate insulin in the blood. Also treats anxiety and depression. Strengthens the memory and increases loyalty and faithfulness, as well as love and passion.

Selenite Clears the mind and assists the use of insight. Promotes accessing of higher consciousness.

Snowy quartz Supports our relinquishing of roles that are no longer appropriate or comfortable, and the liberation of limitations. Helps access deep inner wisdom and enhances tactful behavior and cooperation.

Blue crystals

Celestite, angelite, blue quartz, blue agate, blue tourmaline, turquoise, chrysocolla, sapphire, azurite, lapis lazuli, sodalite

The blue crystals promote calm, harmony and understanding, since they open higher consciousness. They are powerful healing crystals.

Celestite Powerful crystal that aids in spiritual development. Affords contact with the celestial realms and encourages astral travel, dream recall, clairvoyance and spiritual enlightenment. Use to promote balance of mind, and cohesion of intellect and intuition. For healing, celestite can be used for eye and ear ailments and for clearing toxins from the body.

Angelite A form of celestite that has been compacted and compressed, it shares the properties of celestite and is a powerful crystal for use in contacting celestial realms.

Blue quartz Calms fears and facilitates reaching out to others.

Blue agate Increases the vibration of mental energies and facilitates spiritual inspiration and inner peace. Used to treat bone and joint ailments and to strengthen the skeleton, or heal bone fractures. Also used to heal brain fluid imbalances and diseases of the nervous system.

Blue tourmaline Improves psychic awareness and visualization. Used to heal lung and immune system diseases. Opens the third eye chakra.

Turquoise Protects, heals and induces spiritual elation. Offsets negative energies, and promotes healing of spirit and balance of male and female energies. Strengthens creativity in problem-solving. A powerful crystal for healing use for eye ailments.

Chrysocolla Aids meditation. Calms and energizes while improving personal confidence and assisting in speaking the truth. Improves communication skills. Used to treat bone and joint diseases, as well as blood, lung and digestive tract ailments. Can help balance blood sugar levels.

Sapphire The stone of inner peace, serenity and truth. Relaxes the mind, focuses thoughts while releasing mental tension. Promotes balance of mind and clarity of thought. Relieves frustration and confusion, and promotes concentration on control of purpose. One of the good luck crystals, it attracts prosperity and gifts. Treats bleeding, varicose veins, blood disorders, and common viruses such as colds and other respiratory infections.

Azurite Opens the third eye chakra, which strengthens psychic and spiritual abilities and facilitates contact with spiritual guides. Connects with higher consciousness, and effects clear understanding. Stimulates memory and releases communication blocks, opening up the mind to new perspectives. Treats joint problems and alignment of the spinal column.

Lapis lazuli Relieves anger and negative emotions. Improves clarity of expression and opens up channels to inner wisdom. Releases stress and brings peace of mind. Promotes harmony between the physical, emotional, mental and spiritual aspects of the self. Treats headaches, hearing problems, depression, throat and respiratory system, and bone marrow. Strengthens the immune system and relieves insomnia. Good for eyesight problems and strained eyes from computer use.

Sodalite Encourages rationality and objective thought. Bridges between intuition and logic by balancing the emotions. Calms and opens the mind, making it able to absorb new information. Balances metabolism and cleanses organs while boosting the immune system and combating insomnia. Protects against radiation.

Pink crystals

Rose quartz, pink carnelian, danburite, pink tourmaline, kunzite, pink agate, rhodochrosite, moscovite.

The pink crystals are the stones of love, romance and friendship. They are wonderful for healing relationships of all kinds.

Rose quartz The stone of love. Raises self-esteem, teaches self-love and fosters belief in self-worth. Opens the heart chakra, allowing one to receive and accept love. Calms the heart and helps bring about self-forgiveness and self-acceptance. Soothes burns and aids circulatory disorders. Increases fertility. Good for childhood illnesses such as measles and chicken pox. Also heals adult shingles.

Pink carnelian Strengthens relationships between parents and children. Imparts a happy atmosphere, and helps build self-esteem. A grounding stone, it fosters stability in the home and encourages sexuality. Use for allergies and hay fever.

Danburite Eases difficult situations, and fosters patience and peace of mind. Treats the liver and gall bladder, and helps the body gain weight.

Pink tourmaline Cures emotional pain and eliminates destructive emotion. Imparts a feeling of trust and safety in love. Heightens physical and sexual pleasure. Balances the endocrine system. Used as an aphrodisiac, it helps bring love to physical expression.

Kunzite The stone of loving thoughts and spiritual communication, it radiates peace, and connects to universal love. Induces a deep meditative state. Aids in removal of emotional debris and adjusting to pressures in life. Affords tolerance and patience in dealing with circumstances beyond control. Shields and protects from negative energies. Cleanses the aura.

Pink agate Promotes love between parent and child, positive self-image, and personal bravery and confidence. Grounds, and connects to the earth.

Rhodochrosite The stone of unselfishness, compassion, and giving of love. Enhances the dream state, and assimilates painful feelings. Stops denial, and improves feelings of self-worth. Heals asthma, respiratory problems, kidneys, and eyes. Balances thyroid function.

Moscovite Encourages a celestial connection and astral travel. Removes self-doubt and insecurity. Aids in problem solving and use of intuition. Heals blood sugar imbalances and kidney problems.

Yellow crystals

Yellow jade, yellow jasper, citrine, yellow topaz, fluorite, cat's eye, golden beryl

The yellow crystals have strong energies for optimism and forward movement. They attract prosperity, wealth and success while creating an energized and motivated atmosphere. They are good for support during periods of change, and have protective properties both physical and psychic.

Yellow jade A stimulating stone, it energizes and brings joy. Fosters connectedness, harmony and concentration, and supports an atmosphere of meditation.

Yellow jasper Can be used for protection during a trip or move. Supports transformation. Energizes the endocrine system, and increases personal power.

Citrine Supports communication with spiritual guides. Fosters self-confidence.

Citrine is a powerful crystal for attracting prosperity and money. It also aids in the use of intuitive powers, and can be used for healing especially of psychological ills. Citrine is used for setting goals and carrying them through, and for success in new business ventures.

Yellow topaz Used for dealing with episodes of anger, to balance emotions, and to calm the home environment. Protects the home and possessions from intruders and burglars. Strengthens optimism and renews faith.

Fluorite Very protective. Used for counteracting electromagnetic stress. Aids in concentration, and heightens intuition. Stimulates sexual desire, and enhances creativity. Useful for healing teeth, bones, and joint ailments. Used for "changing luck." Can be used for divination and scrying (crystal-gazing). Strengthens psychic powers.

Cat's eye A good luck stone. Promotes confidence and happiness, while helping the user to become "grounded." It possesses strong protective properties and attracts prosperity. Cat's eye also supports healing of eye and vision disorders, as well as headaches and facial pain.

Golden beryl Very supportive of psychic abilities and the connection to other realms. Opens the crown chakra and promotes purity of intention. Strengthens initiative and independence.

Orange crystals

Carnelian, orange calcite, orange jade, orange celestite

The orange crystals help with organization of thought and action, and with taking control of situations. They increase personal power, and facilitate change of luck.

Carnelian Imparts bravery, protection, strength, and self-confidence. Associated with the lower chakras. Used for grounding and connecting to sexual energies. Helps remove the fear of death, and brings about acceptance of the cycles of life. Can be used for motivation to success. Used for healing back pain, joint pain, and depression.

Orange calcite The stone of happiness and energetic lust for life. Imparts a feeling of joy and well-being. Strengthens sexual energies, and helps dream recall. Maximizes potential and helps remove obstacles.

Orange jade Releases negative thoughts and brings harmony and serenity. Aids in finding answers in dreams. Used to cure kidney disease and to heal cuts and wound.

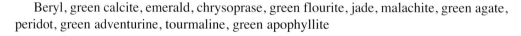

Orange celestite Helps attract good fortune. (See blue celestite above.)

Green crystals

Beryl, green calcite, emerald, chrysoprase, green flourite, jade, malachite, green agate, peridot, green adventurine, tourmaline, green apophyllite

The green crystals strengthen the balance energies, especially in marriage and relationships. The green crystals also promote fertility and growth and foster creativity and financial prosperity.

Beryl Aids memory, relieves stress, and calms the mind. Good for concentration filters out distractions. Heals pulmonary, circulation, and excretory systems. Also treats the throat, liver, heart, stomach, spine and skull (concussion).

Green calcite Promotes balance and mental healing. Brings out truth and enhances spiritual awareness. Use to purify the body and heal infections.

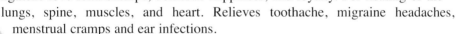

Emerald For emotional and physical balance and equilibrium. Fosters positive intention and subsequent action. Promotes deep, inner knowing and spiritual awareness. Energizes the heart chakra and draws out talents and abilities. Strengthens love relationships, domestic happiness, and loyalty. For healing of the lungs, spine, muscles, and heart. Relieves toothache, migraine headaches, menstrual cramps and ear infections.

Chrysoprase Releases the energies surrounding an issue. Supports creativity, hope, and eloquence. Releases ego energy, and encourages peace and relaxation. Aids in treatment of gout, eye problems, and mental illness.

Green fluorite Calms excess energy and promotes serenity. Heals emotional trauma. Clears infections and aids stomach upsets and intestinal disorders.

Jade Induces a relaxing atmosphere and calms the nervous system. Symbol of harmony in relationships and purity of thoughts. Soothes the mind by releasing negative thoughts. Said to be the stone of longevity, it protects vitality and channels passions constructively. Balances the female hormonal systems. Use for fertility problems and menstrual irregularity.

Malachite Said to be the stone of vitality and transformation, it breaks unwanted ties and loosens the hold of old relationships and behaviors and fosters the taking of responsibility for one's own life. Encourages patience and tolerance. Helps clarify emotions and releases negative past experiences. Used for treating asthma, fractures, growths and tumors.

Green agate Strengthens personal defenses, and increases self-esteem. Clears negative energies from the body and spirit. Used for eliminating unwanted habits such as smoking. Supports decision-making abilities and helps resolve disputes.

Peridot Alleviates negative energies and promotes clarity and well-being. Reduces stress, and supports change and growth. Said to attract money and financial abundance. Used for healing the heart, lungs, spleen, and as an aid in childbirth.

Green adventurine Creates an atmosphere of success, optimism, and good luck. Supports creative endeavors, and fosters good communication.

Tourmaline Defeats dark spells against one. Balances energies. Attracts inspiration and supports creative and artistic enterprises. Helps release guilt. Attracts money and wealth. A particularly strong crystal for personal protection, and is used to heal immune system disorders, nervous system problems, eye and heart disease.

Green apophyllite Provides peace, calm and clarity. The universal "love stone," it promotes self-acceptance, forthrightness, and serenity of mind.

Purple crystals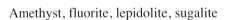

Amethyst, fluorite, lepidolite, sugalite

The purple crystals foster spiritual growth and connection. They are used to break bad luck and to strengthen psychic powers.

Amethyst A powerful crystal for healing and protection. Enhances psychic abilities and clears the aura. Calms the mind and facilitates meditation. Protects against psychic attack, and calms anger, rage, fear and resentment. Eases grief, sadness, and yearning.

Relieves physical pain, and heals cellular disorders, hearing loss, and nervous system ills. Boosts hormone production.

Fluorite Relaxes the mind. Enhances memory and concentration. Heals teeth and gums, and eases back pain.

Lepidolite Strengthens the connection with higher consciousness, stops over-active thinking and reduces mental tension. Stimulates cosmic awareness and opens the third eye chakra. Protects against electromagnetic stress. Treats insomnia and sleep disturbances, as well as the symptoms of menopause.

Sugalite Like the pink stones, sugalite is a "love crystal." Promotes positive thinking, channeling ability, and spiritual awareness. Allows forgiveness, and eases hostile thoughts. Aids learning difficulties and autism. Supports group cooperation and harmony, and acceptance of social outcasts. Aids headache sufferers.

Black crystals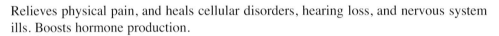

Obsidian, jet, sardonyx, onyx, black tourmaline

The black crystals repel and transform negative spells and thoughts into positive energy. They reverse black magic.

Obsidian Used for breaking bad habits, attracting success in business, and setting and accomplishing goals. Improves self-control. Defeats black magic or demonic possession. Good during periods of grief and for eliminating negative energy. A very strong crystal, it should not be used for long periods.

 Jet Protects against violence and stabilizes the environment. Draws out unreasonable fears and negative thoughts for transmutation. Calms mood swings and fights depression. Protects financial stability. Use to treat migraines, swellings, and epilepsy, and to increase virility.

Sardonyx Absorbs negativity and clears negative energies. Used for absorbing and removing unwanted energies.

Onyx Calms the atmosphere and the mind. Can be used to reverse and defeat black magic or to repel evil. Should be used when trying to kick a habit or end an addiction such as to alcohol or drugs. Enhances creativity and inspiration, and balances the mind, promoting spiritual awareness. Supports good luck and longevity.

Black tourmaline Protective stone. Repels microwaves and radiation. Reverses negative spells of ill-wishers. Strengthens the immune system and treats arthritis.

Brown crystals

Amber, tiger's eye, topaz, brown agates, smoky quartz, jasper

The brown crystals ground and strengthen the connection to the earth. They increase common sense and psychic abilities.

Amber Used to draw impurities from the body. Promotes, patience, wisdom, and balance. Eases stress and cleanses the mind and spirit. Aids decision-making. Heals breathing ailments such as asthma and bronchitis.

 Tiger's eye Encourages proper use of inner strength and resources. Aids decision-making and accomplishment. Clarifies intention and goals.

Integrates change and balances the body's energies. Enhances psychic connection.

Topaz Recharges and directs energies. Increases motivation and energy. Promotes vibrant health, generosity, and joy.

Brown agates These stones deepen the connection with the earth and strengthen sexual energies. They calm the mind and promote introspective thought while releasing mental blocks and dispelling fear. Use to treat stomach problems and central nervous system disorders, as well as eye and vision problems.

Smoky quartz Detoxifies the body and aids elimination. Encourages a calm mind and uplifting thoughts. Protective during radiation or chemotherapy. Neutralizes negative influences.

Jasper A stone of nurturing and protection, jasper grounds and invites tranquillity. Aids organizational skills and facilitates agile thinking. Opens the base chakra and prolongs sexual pleasure.

Transparent crystals

Quartz, diamond

The clear crystals are some of the strongest energetically. They heighten the connection to psychic forces and amplify the effects of other stones.

Quartz Transparent quartz crystals are very powerful stones. They can be used to purify and strengthen the energies of other crystals. They are energy regulators, and can clean and regulate the aura field of people and objects.

Enhance psychic awareness and abilities. Used together with other crystals, they magnify their energies.

Diamond The stone of purity and clarity, diamonds symbolize love and deep spiritual connection. Aids in acquisition of courage, fortitude, and bravery. Heals the immune system and strengthens the effects of chemotherapy and radiotherapy.

Red crystals

Red calcite, garnet, ruby, aventurine, red jasper
The red crystals impart a feeling of increased energy and vitality, and encourage action. They impart confidence in the face of a test or conflict.

Red calcite Increases vitality and encourages positive emotion.Increases self-confidence.

Garnet An energizing and revitalizing stone, it also brings about balance and serenity. Treats spinal disorders and blood and lung problems. Regenerates DNA. Helps with absorption of vitamins and minerals. Controls self-directed anger. Can be used to activate other crystals.

Ruby The crystal associated with cardiac health. Associated with sexuality, pregnancy and childbirth. Energizes and stimulates and encourages the opening of the heart chakra. Promotes retaining of wealth and possessions. Treats fever and blood flow. Aids recovery after stroke or heart attack.

Aventurine Eases worries. Relieves pain. Releases negative energies. Brings about feelings of joy and encourages good luck and success. Enhances creativity, and helps in discerning new opportunities. Heals skin problems and balances blood pressure.

Red jasper Ground energies. Helps with dream recall and rebirthing process. Can be used to rectify unjust situations. Heals disorders of the circulatory system.

Preparing crystals for candle magic

The crystals you use should be your own, and purified to work with your energy. This means you must not borrow a crystal, or use a crystal which has been worn for decoration by someone else or which has performed some other function.

After you buy your crystal, or receive it as a gift, it is very important to purify it before using it for magic. There are several ways this can be done. The simplest cleansing is done under running water. You can use your bathroom or kitchen faucet. Simply hold the crystal under the free-flowing water for several minutes, and then set it out to dry naturally in the sun. If the water in your home is particularly mineral rich (hard water), you might rinse it under flowing distilled water instead.

Another powerful method of purification is the use of salt water. If you live near the ocean, you can put your crystal into a bowl of seawater for an hour, and then rinse it with clear fresh water. Salt water can be prepared at home by dissolving rock salt in tap water or distilled water. Let the crystal soak for a few hours, rinse, and air dry, preferably in the sun.

Some crystals are fragile and will not tolerate purification with water. If you can easily dislodge crystal "dust" when running your fingers across your crystal, you have one that should not be rinsed or soaked in water.

These crystals can be purified in salt alone. Simply bury the crystal in a bowl of salt for a few hours or overnight.

After cleansing, you are almost ready to use your crystal in your magic ritual. However, another important step, which will further energize your crystal for its purpose, is dedication. With this process, you inform your crystal exactly what it is you wish it to do for you. You will infuse the crystal with your intentions, which will align its vibrations with the vibration of your desire, making it an even more powerful partner to your candle magic. After dedication, your crystal remains charged with your intention until you purify or rededicate it.

Simply cradle the crystal in your hands, and think carefully about the declared goal for your magic. Utter your goal aloud, using very precise language, so as not to confuse the crystal and create a counterproductive energy. You can ask your crystal to attract something positive or to repel something you don't want in your life. The crystal can focus its energies and communicate electromagnetically according to your programming, so be careful what intention you communicate to it.

Incense

Like crystals, incense has been used for centuries in conjunction with ceremonial rituals of all types. Incense was thought to have psychoactive properties that brought about contact with supernatural forces. In pre-biblical times, perfumes and incense were considered quite precious and often the dead were honored by being buried with fragrant substances in order to cajole the gods into granting them immortality. In the ancient Greek culture, incense was offered to the gods in return for favors, and Greek mythology is rich

in references to aromatic substances. Many bronze and gold incense burners have been found by archeologists in the ruins of ancient temples, where it is assumed that incense was used during religious celebrations and rites.

The infusion of scent into the atmosphere can greatly enhance the candle magic. The aroma can help transform the energies in the room while we prepare for the magic to take place. Via the sense of smell, we are easily transported to another dimension of thought and feeling, opening us up to the possibilities of our own higher powers.

Several types of incense are readily available for purchase. Combustible incense, which can be burned directly, is probably the most common and easiest to use. It can be found in the form of sticks or cones, which burn easily and evenly. It is important to burn incense in a proper holder or ceramic bowl filled with sand, since its ash will fall as the incense is consumed.

Choose your incense to balance the atmosphere according to the magic you wish to perform, or choose all-purpose incense that will enhance any mood or magic, such as frankincense or sandalwood. Your sense of smell will tell you if an aroma suits you and your magic.

(Aubrey Beardsley)

The following is a general guide to choosing incense and oil fragrances according to their healing and magical properties.

Apple Happiness, peace and harmony. Friendship and romantic love.

Acacia Enhances meditation, visualizing, divination, and clairvoyance.

Amber Comfort, happiness, love, healing.

Ambergris Opens the crown chakra, and enhances psychic powers.

Bayberry Good luck and fortune. Realization of wishes, happiness, and prosperity. Justice.

Bergamot Money, wealth, and spiritual uplifting.

Carnation Healing, physical strength, self-defense and protection. Love and lust.

Cedar Purification and cleansing, attracting money, healing, removal of hexes.

Cinnamon Meditation, purification and cleansing, protection and defense, healing, power and strength, good fortune, and justice. Stimulates business success. Divination and clairvoyance.

Citronella Protection and defense, cleansing. Strong scent not for indoor use.

Clove Relief of pain, wealth and prosperity, business success, release or banishing of something, peace and harmony, wisdom and inspiration, psychic awareness and divination.

Cypress Peace, harmony, and serenity. Protective and binding. Heals and comforts.

Dragon's blood Powerful and protective. Use to increase the power of any other scent and to add strength to any spell or ritual.

Eucalyptus Eases nasal and lung congestion. For purifying and protection.

Frankincense Spirituality, connection to astral spheres, courage, protection, consecration and blessing.

Gardenia Healing, peace, and love.

Ginger Invigorating and strengthening. Attracts wealth, love, success and power.

Jasmine Happiness and harmony. Protection and defense. Astral projection, money, and love. Wisdom and skills.

Juniper Love, happiness and peace. Protection and defense. Calming and healing.

Lavender Purification and cleansing. Calmness, relaxation, and healing. Love and harmony.

Lilac Happiness and joy. To ward something off. Soothing. Divination.

Lotus Healing, strength, power. Meditation and spirituality. Lifts moods.

Mint Good fortune. Justice. Changes. Cleansing.

Myrrh Healing, meditation, consecration, spirituality. Purification.

Patchouli Warmth and sensuality, growth, love.

Peppermint Healing, cleansing, mental stimulation. Increases energies.

Pine Grounding, cleansing, healing, strength.

Rose Love, happiness, peace and harmony, healing, fertility. Divination and clairvoyance.

Rosemary Exorcism, healing, remembrance. Will power. Happiness and joy.

Sage Wisdom, inspiration, and clarity. Exorcism and purification.

Sandalwood Spirituality, healing, astral projection, and exorcism.

Strawberry Love and good luck.

Vanilla Mental power, love.

Vervain Release and banishing. Creativity, good luck, and justice.

Vetivert Removal of hexes. Money and prosperity. Love, happiness, and harmony.

Violet Healing, protection, and wisdom. Love, good luck, and fortune.

Wisteria Psychic abilities.

Ylang-Ylang Joy, love, harmony, and peace.

Oils

Oils are used in the preparation of candles for use in magic. Natural oils, like incense, strengthen the magic with their particular properties, frequencies and fragrances. Choose oils according to their magical properties, and/or according to your Zodiac sign. If you are using a Zodiac candle, you can use the appropriate oil to magnify its significance. You can also use the oil appropriate to your sign on another candle in your ritual. Try to obtain pure oil that is extracted directly from the plant or fruit. This kind of oil is called an essential oil. Some essential oils can be purchased and used in their purest form, and others are prepared commercially using carrier oils, which make it possible to work with some essences which would be too harsh or powerful undiluted. Store your oils in tightly closed dark bottles, away from children. Some can be harmful if ingested or when coming into contact with the skin in high concentrations.

The following lists of oils and their corresponding signs and properties will help you choose the right oils to prepare your candles for magic.

Oils and their properties for magic:

Oils according to the Zodiac:

Aries: Cedar, pine

Taurus: Rose, geranium

Gemini: Lavender, lemongrass

Cancer: Jasmine, sandalwood

Leo: Juniper, orange flower

Virgo: Patchouli, lily

Libra: Marjoram, magnolia

Scorpio: Myrrh, lemon balm

Sagittarius: Rosemary, frankincense

Capricorn: Cyprus, vetivert

Aquarius: Lemon verbena, coriander

Pisces: Ylang-ylang, chamomile

Amber: Love, happiness, comfort, healing

Apple blossom: Friendship, love, happiness

Bayberry: Prosperity, protection, control

Bergamot: Optimism, attracting money and prosperity, happiness

Carnation: Protection, healing, love, strength

Cedar: Purification, protection, attracting money, removal of hexes

Cinnamon: Stimulation, prosperity, success in business, energy, healing

Clove: Success in business, wealth and prosperity, protection, psychic awareness, creativity, intellectual stimulation

Cypress: Healing, comfort

Eucalyptus: Healing, purification, protection, relief of nasal and lung congestion

Frankincense: Spirituality, purification, protection, consecration, courage

Gardenia: Peace, love, healing, happiness, harmony

Ginger: Wealth, invigoration, lust, love

Hibiscus: Divination, love

Honeysuckle: Psychic powers, money, friendship, healing, happiness

Jasmine: Encourages psychic dreams, fantasy, purification, wisdom, skills, astral projection, love, money

Juniper: Healing, protection, calmness

Lavender: Happiness, cleansing, love, healing

Lemon: Purification, healing, love

Lemongrass: Psychic powers, mental clarity

Lilac: Protection, warding off evil, exorcism

Lotus: Spirituality, mood elevation, opening, healing, meditation, protection, purification

Magnolia: Trees, nature, oneness, hair growth

Musk: Attracts opposite sex, aphrodisiac, prosperity

Myrrh: Protection, spirituality, hex-breaking, meditation, healing, consecration

Orange: Divination, luck, love, money, psychic powers

Patchouli: Love, growth, mastery, warmth and sensuality

Pennyroyal: Purification

Peppermint: Stimulation, energy, healing, creativity, money

Pine: Strength, grounding, cleansing and purification, protection, exorcism, healing

Rose: Fertility, love, healing, cleansing and blessing of home or room

Rosemary: Energy, protection, healing, remembrance

Sage: Wisdom, clarity, purification, truth

Sandalwood: Healing, protection, astral projection, exorcism, spirituality

Vanilla: Lust, mental powers

Vetiver: Removal of hexes, peace, money, love

Violet: Wisdom, luck, love, healing

Yarrow: Courage, psychic powers, exorcism

Ylang-Ylang: Love, harmony, happiness

H e r b s

In almost every culture, herbs have long played a part in healing, and various herbs have been associated with magical powers and mystical uses as well.

Use of herbs can enhance your magic and make it more powerful, especially if you choose one that is compatible to your magic goal.

Like incense and oils, herbs should be chosen according to the type of magic ritual you are performing, and the energetic properties of the individual herbs. The herbs used can be fresh perhaps grown in your own garden or window sill or dried (even herbs sold in the spice section of the supermarket will do). Whichever you use, they should be new and unused prior to the magic.

Store-bought herbs can be passed through the smoke of sage incense to purify them and erase any negative energy they may have acquired in previous handling. Fresh herbs should be rinsed in salt water and dried thoroughly.

Herbs which have been finely crushed can be added to the hot wax when making candles. Alternatively, they can be added to a candle by rolling the anointed candle in crushed herbs just before burning. As part of your ritual, herbs can be burned directly on small charcoal blocks acquired for this purpose. Note that many of the herbs can also be burned in the form of incense, and correspond to the properties of the incense of the same name above.

The herbs listed here have powerful magic properties There is a virtually infinite variety of herbs, so this list is necessarily quite selective. Choose carefully, and remember that it is not always necessary to add herbs to your ritual. Follow your intuition.

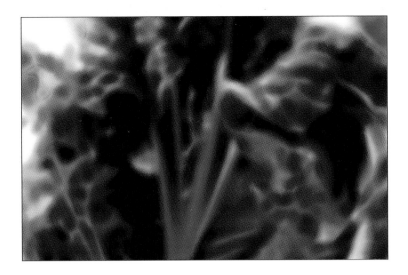

Herbs and their magical influences

Barley Pain relief.

Basil Joy, love, courage, and healing. Enhances psychic powers. Protects the home, deters theft. Fosters a peaceful environment, and clears the air after a quarrel. Also used for purification, healing, and vitality

Bracken For pleasant dreams and peaceful sleep.

Bay laurel Stops interference and protects against evil influence.

Catnip Love, happiness, courage.

Chamomile Calms, brings luck in games of chance, attracts a mate.

Cinnamon Success, motivation, stimulation.

Citronella Past life regression, protection, astral travel.

Clove Attracts abundance, helps in realizing a material desire.

Dragon's blood Drives away evil influences, removes hexes and protects strongly. Also good for money and love spells.

Eucalyptus leaves Healing.

Frankincense Purification, spiritual journey, protection.

Ginger Money and success, power, love.

High John the Conqueror Good fortune, lifting of spirits.

Jasmine Psychic and mental abilities, love, money.

Juniper Protection, love.

Lavender Love, money, relaxation and calm. Balance, peace, and attracting helping spirits.

Lemon verbena Repels evil, rebuffs unwanted suitors.

Lily of the valley Peace, knowledge.

Marigold Promotes clairvoyant dreams.

Mistletoe Healing, pleasant dreams, ends despair, protection from theft.

Mugwort Strengthens psychic and divination abilities.

Myrrh Purification, protection, spiritual abilities.

Nutmeg Luck in gambling, love, fertility, prosperity.

Oak Abundance, fertility, protection, spiritual awareness.

Patchouli Money, rekindling lost love, defeating enemies.

Peppermint Increases psychic ability, love, purification.

Pine Purification.

Tempus erit.

Rose Love, peace, happiness, healing of heart ailments.

Rosemary Fidelity, healing, exorcism. Strengthens memory and encourages comforting memories of the deceased.

Rue Repels negativity, hexes and bad spells. Attracts love.

Sage Purification, wisdom, protection, elimination of negative energy from environment.

Spearmint Prosperity, money, ease during travel, protection, and healing.

St. John's Wort Healing, happiness, courage, love, protection. Divination.

Sandalwood Protection, spirituality, realization of wishes.

Thyme Cleanses the aura, prevents nightmares.

Vervain Repels psychic attack. Purification, love, wealth.

Yarrow Divination, love, happy marriage.

Timing your candle magic

Choosing the best time for your magic ritual can greatly enhance the energies available to make your goals a reality. Using the lunar cycle as your basic guide, you can choose the optimum day and time for your magic. The phases of the moon have a powerful effect on all systems on Earth, and influence the way we function in our daily lives. The planets nearest to Earth also exert a strong force, and knowledge of this can be harnessed to help us succeed in candle magic.

In general, when the moon is waxing (while it is "growing"), it is the correct time for magic connected to the beginning of new ventures, wealth and prosperity, growth and building of any kind, and for love. The waxing moon begins when the moon is new, and continues until the full moon. Magic aimed at bringing something into your life should be performed during this period.

The full moon the 24-hour period when the moon is at its largest and brightest is the most powerful time of the lunar cycle. Magic for attracting money, success, love, or growth goals of any kind will be reinforced when performed during the period when the moon is full. This kind of magic can be successful at other times during the waxing moon, but the full moon is the strongest.

The waning moon cycle begins the day after the full moon and continues until the next new moon. During this period, magic for repelling or removing anything unwanted should be performed. Breaking bad habits, gaining protection from anything that is negative, and terminating unwanted relationships should be done during the period of the waning moon. When the moon is dark – the 24-hour period when no light is reflected off the moon – it is the most powerful period for spells of removal or repelling.

In addition to the phase of the moon, you may wish to identify the day of the week most conducive to your magic by considering the planetary as well as the solar influences. The planets, sun and moon are each most powerful on a particular day of the week. They are also associated with certain influences on our lives, and thus on our magic. The powers of each are complimented by the addition of particular crystals and herbs. The following chart will help you pinpoint the best day for your magic. Bear in mind, however, that magic can be successful on any day or hour. These are simply guidelines for maximizing your results.

Day of the Week

Heavenly Body
Magic Powers
Incense, oils, and herbs
Crystals
Colors

Monday

Fertility   Divination   Moon

Luck   Calming emotions   Love

Myrtle, mugwort, jasmine, lotus   Moonstone, clear quartz crystal, pearl

Dreams

Silver, gray, white, pale blue

Tuesday

Mars

Surgery

Strength

Courage

Athletics

Defense

Red   Dragon's blood

Bloodstone, garnet, ruby

Protection

Wednesday

Creativity   Business   Mercury

Orange, violet   Writing   Memory

Sandalwood

Divination

Carnelian, agate, fire opal

Thursday

Honor   Jupiter

Legal matters

Purple, royal blue

Lapus lazuli, amethyst, sapphire   Family

Luck

Employment success

Cedar, nutmeg, lilac

Friday

Pregnancy

Harmony   Love   Venus

Fertility   Pink, pale blue, green

Children   Amber, malachite, jade, peridot, emerald

Marriage

Friendship   Musk, verbena, rose, sandalwood

Saturday

Saturn

Binding

Knowledge

Protection

Black, dark blue, dark
purple, dark brown

Poppy, myrrh

Onyx, jet, star
sapphire

Finding lost objects

Influencing others, collecting
debts, removing obstacles

Sunday

Hope

Sun

Promotion

Prosperity

Healing

Happiness

Yellow topaz, yellow
diamond, goldstone, zircon

Success

Gold, deep yellow

Clove, cinnamon, musk, vanilla,
orange blossom, frankincense

(Aubrey Beardsley)

If you wish to be even more accurate in timing your magic, you can choose a time of day according to the energies which are most strongly at play. Morning is the optimal time for healing rituals and for the release of negative impulses and forces. Morning is also best for purification rituals and consecration. Noontime is the time of day when energies are strongest and most forceful. Rituals involving the attraction of abundance and the desire for courage, strength and protection should be performed around noon. Evening is a good time for rituals involving banishing undesirable elements. Breaking bad habits, undoing hexes, and dispelling negative energies are most effective in the evening. Nighttime is best for rituals concerning contact with the psychic realms, attracting positive dreams, love rituals, and divination.

Some candle magic practitioners choose a time according to the hands of the clock. For magic intended to bring something into your life, the ritual would take place when both hands of the clock are on the rise (that is, during the second half of any hour between 6 am and noon, or between 6 pm and midnight). For magic intended to repel or terminate, the first half of the hours between 12 midnight and 6 am or between 12 noon and 6 pm (when both hands of the clock are on the way down) would be optimal.

Additional considerations when choosing the best time for your magic are your own physical and emotional states. Some practitioners advise abstaining from magic when in a sexually depleted state (males) or during menstruation. It is also advisable to let any open wounds heal completely before attempting a magic ritual. In order to imbue the magic with optimal energies, you need to be as rested and strong as possible. Do not try to perform magic while in an acutely depressed or manic state. If you take drugs or other medications, you may want to have someone else perform your ritual, or at the very least, perform your magic when you are at the end of a dosage period, and therefore have the smallest amount of medicine in your system. And of course, do not attempt a ritual when you are under the influence of narcotics or alcohol.

All this does not mean that you cannot perform a ritual aimed at acquiring more strength, getting rid of an illness, or kicking a bad habit. It just means you must try to find the optimal physical condition and frame of mind in order to make your magic as powerful as possible.

Magic spells

What does the phrase "magic spell" conjure up in your imagination? Perhaps you think of a witch toiling over a steaming cauldron or a thick book of incantations that must be memorized precisely in order to work inexplicable wonders. Maybe you believe that there are particular words or word sequences that in and of themselves release a power that does magic. These beliefs about spells are only partly true.

In the Oxford English Dictionary, the word "spell" is defined as "A set of words, a formula or verse, supposed to possess occult or magical powers; a charm or incantation; a means of accomplishing enchantment or exorcism."

What has been omitted from this definition and most others is the intent of the person casting the spell. It is very important to understand that the words alone have no power. They derive their power from the intent and the concentration of thought of the person casting the spell. The magic begins with your thoughts and your belief that you can bring about the desired result by getting the forces of energy that exist in the universe to work for you via your magic ritual. The spell is simply the verbal expression of your desire. The words are the expression of your intent in language. They have no power save the power of your thoughts and beliefs – which is formidable! Magic is powered by thought. Concentrated thought emits a powerful energy, even before it is put into words. Then the words help you direct that energy and keep it focused.

The spell begins with your imagination. Your mind visualizes your desire. Then this visualization engenders a feeling, an emotion, within you. By feeling your desired outcome, and by living it in your mind as if it has already come about, you begin to focus on the proper energy for your magic. At this point, you are ready to formulate a spell – that is, to put into words your thoughts and feelings about your desire.

Some magic practitioners advocate meditation before writing a spell. You can try this if you think it will help you clear your mind and bring forth only that which is related to your magic. If you don't wish to or don't know how to meditate, simply find a quiet spot to focus your thoughts on the desired result of your magic. Try to imagine yourself already having achieved your desire. Ask yourself very specifically what it is that you desire. The more clearly and specifically you can define your goal, the more powerful your spell will be. Do not say "I want to be healthy." Instead, state that "my asthma is gone – I breathe clearly and freely at all times." Rather than saying "I don't want a divorce," say "My marriage is strong and happy. My partner and I share an abiding love and commitment."

If you feel embroiled in many problems in life, try to concentrate on them one at a time. Magic that is directed at "solving all my problems" will be diffuse and lacking in direction. Choose one area and affirm specifically the outcome you want. If you want to attract more prosperity, be sure you wish for it honestly, and not at the expense of another person, or as a result of tragedy, accident, or criminal wrongdoing. Never try to control another person's actions. This includes asking for a specific person to become attracted to you. Instead, ask for "a wonderful love to come into my life" or to "find the perfect mate." Trust in the universe to find the optimal means for your goal to be realized. Imagine the outcome in great detail, but not the path leading to it.

Ask yourself how you will feel in the new reality. Then try to feel yourself already there. This feeling is the most important element of the spell. If you cannot bring yourself to feel what it will be like to have realized your desire, you will not emit the proper vibrations, and the words of your spell will have little power. Visualize and feel this way for several minutes. Then, put pen to paper, and express your visualization in words.

Think of your spell as a type of wishful thinking, or as a kind of prayer. See yourself giving verbal instructions to the universe about what it is you want to realize in your life.

You need not be a talented writer to create a powerful spell. Your spell needn't rhyme, unless this comes naturally to you, is pleasing to you, or seems to you to make your spell more powerful. Don't worry about whether the spell sounds impressive or if it has a "magical" ring to it. Use language that contains the feeling of your intent. Usually this will be language made up of words you normally use in your daily life, and not esoteric language with which you are not comfortable. Your spell does not have to be of any particular length. Sometimes the shortest spells are the most powerful.

Once you have written your spell, you will have infused those particular words with your intent. They will remain charged until you use the spell in your magic.

What about "ready-made" spells you found in a book such as this or in another source? If you find a spell that seems to fit your intention and with which you feel comfortable and identify, you can certainly use it. You will be able to feel if the words coincide with your feelings regarding your magic goal. Simply practice the spell several times before your magic ritual until it becomes a part of you, change it a bit if necessary, and make it compatible with your visualization and feeling of your goal. You might find that reading examples of spells will open your mind to the process and your own spells will flow more easily.

Performing the candle magic ritual

Once you have written your spell, you must choose your ritual materials.

Candles, oil, and incense are vital elements. The others are optional.

Choose carefully, according to the objective of your magic.

The candle ritual you use for your magic can be one you have found in a book such as this, or it can be invented by you, according to what you have learned about the elements of candle magic. If you decide to use a "ready-made" ritual, you can always modify it to suit your own needs, so that it feels comfortable and right for you. You may want to use more or fewer candles, or add more crystals or herbs, or write a different spell, for example.

Your ritual does not need to be elaborate or complicated. You may choose to use just one candle, incense, and oil. Your magic can still be effective. You might want to start off with simple rituals until you become comfortable with performing candle magic.

The information in this book can be your guide, and it can help you to fashion an infinite variety of candle magic rituals to serve your purposes. For each magic goal, devote some time and thought to gathering the proper candles and materials. Be sure the colors, scents, and other elements match your present goal.

It is vital to remember that your magic will only be as powerful as the strength of your thoughts and beliefs. You must believe that the lighting of the candle and the performing of the ritual are powerful tools to effect change and provide answers for you. The power of your belief combined with the natural power of the fire element will make the magic work. Without your concentration, visualization, and intent, the effect of the magic will be weaker. Never try to do more than one ritual at a time, since your thoughts will be too diffuse, and each ritual will be weakened.

Begin to put yourself in the frame of mind for magic by cleaning the area and taking a shower or bath. Make sure you are free from distractions, and focus on the magic about to take place. Try to remain undistracted until you are finished with your spell. Turn your phone off or have someone else answer it, and have small children supervised elsewhere.

Visualize your room and especially the area of your altar bathed in white light and free of any kind of negative energy. Many candle magic practitioners meditate before performing magic. You may want to put on some soft instrumental music in the background.

Prepare your altar in an esthetic and pleasing manner. Set out your materials and any decorative items such as a vase of flowers, a small statue of a deity, or perhaps a picture. Be sure you have all of the necessary tools for your magic close at hand.

Begin by lighting the altar candle. You may use a sulfur match or lighter, or you may prefer to bring the flame into the room using a small white candle you have lit elsewhere.

As you perform your ritual, you will use the flame of the altar candle to light all of the other candles. A small white candle may be used to carry the flame of the altar candle to each candle used for the magic. Alternatively, you can light each candle with a separate match [E: this contradicts previous] or lighter. This is according to your preference, and there are conflicting beliefs on this. Use your intuition, and light your candles in the manner with which you feel most comfortable.

Your helping materials should be added to the ritual in a way that is esthetically pleasing to you. Alternatively, follow the guidelines in the sample rituals in this book. Generally, the incense is lit along with the altar candle, and is placed in the rear area of the altar. If you are burning herbs, light them after the altar candle and incense have been lit.

Next, prepare your candles by anointing them with the oil you have chosen.

If you wish, you may use several oils – a different one for each candle – according to their properties and the goal of your magic. Wash your hands carefully and calm your mind before beginning to anoint your candles.

Anointing (sometimes called dressing) is done slowly and deliberately, using the fingers only. If you seek to bring something into your life, use a beckoning motion for anointing your candle. In other words, place a few drops of oil on your fingertips, and rub them from the wick of the candle to the end. Try to cover the candle with oil, but you do not have to use a large amount. If you wish to repel or remove something from your life, anoint the candle in the opposite direction, rubbing from end to wick. If you are using a large or tall candle, you can anoint the upper and lower halves of the candle, one at a time. Using this method, rub the oil downward from the wick to the middle, and downward again from the middle to the end when you want to attract something. When you wish to repel, terminate, or remove something, rub the oil from the middle of the candle to the wick, and then from the middle to the end. If you are working with a glass-encased candle, anoint the top of the candle with a circular clockwise motion of your fingertips to attract, and rub counter clockwise to repel.

Carefully and slowly anoint your candle, keeping your magic goal foremost in your mind. Focus your concentration during the anointing. Think of the desired result of your magic. Try not to let your mind wander. Consciously infuse the candle with your energy while visualizing your optimal result. This will charge your candle with your intentions for the magic.

Repeat until each candle you are using for your ritual has been anointed and energized with the proper frequencies.

You may wish to inscribe the candles you are using with specific symbols or words that represent your magic goal. You can use any delicate sharp object for this task, such as a pin, a small knife blade, or a small nail. You can inscribe the candle with your astrological sign, a small picture of your desired outcome if you are able, or with other symbols that are meaningful to you. If you want to attract something to your life, inscribe its symbol on the top half of the candle, drawing or writing from the top toward the middle. To send something away or repel it from your life, write or draw from the middle, downward toward the end of the candle. As you work, visualize the outcome, and speak it out loud. Keep the inscriptions simple and focused, and use each candle for only one purpose at a time. Remember that as you prepare your candles to perform your magic ritual, your thoughts are paving the way for success. Stay focused on your magic goals.

Wishes can also be inscribed on a sheet of paper rather than directly onto the candle. Write your question or desired outcome on a slip of paper to be placed under the candle before burning. Alternatively, you may burn the paper as part of your ritual after lighting the candles for magic. Using paper of a color significant to your magic will strengthen the effect.

Once your candles are ready, place them on the altar in the pattern prescribed in your ritual. If you are using a ritual of your own invention, simply place the candles in a way that seems logical to you. For example, if the aim of the ritual is to improve a relationship, place the candles representing the parties in the relationship close to one another, side by side. If there are candles representing people, or astrological candles in your ritual, place them in front of the altar candle, with other candles being used for the magic in front and to the side.

Light your candles for the magic, and chant your spell. Repeat the spell several times, if you feel so inclined. Again, use your own intuition, and you will know when you have finished saying what you want to say. Chant your spell in a clear and loud voice, gazing at the flames of the candles.

After you have finished, sit near the altar for a short period, thinking about your desired outcome. You may then leave the altar unattended, but it is advisable to check periodically to make sure the candles are burning safely, and it is never a good idea to leave the house. If something comes up to prevent you from supervising the candles, simply snuff them out and begin your magic again later. (In this case you can use the same candles again, provided that they have not been disturbed in the meantime.) If a candle goes out on its own during the magic, do not relight it – rather, consider that candle to be finished for this ritual, and dispose of it after the others have burned down.

The altar candle(s) should remain lit until the candles for magic have completely burned down and the ritual is over. They should then be snuffed out. You may want to purify the altar candles before their next use, and they should never be burned for any other purpose. If you have a permanent altar, the altar candles can be lit when you are not performing magic, however.

When the candles for magic have burned down, the ritual is over, and it is advisable to clean up as soon as possible. Dispose of the ash from the incense, paper or herbs you have burned, as well as the leftover wax. For magic you wish to repeat, always begin the next day with a clean altar and fresh candles and other materials.

And be sure to keep in mind that like any skill, magic takes practice. Some people are more naturally attuned and can perform successful magic the first time, and for others it may take some fine-tuning and experience. Don't give up. We all have the capacity for real magic.

Candle magic rituals for petition

Petition simply refers to asking for something. You might be asking for something to happen or for some type of change or growth to occur.

Asking for something to be removed from your life is also a form of petition. The following are some examples of petitioners' rituals in several main areas of the life path.

Candle magic for relationships

Attracting a mate:

Rituals for attracting a mate should never be directed at a specific person. Instead, foster the intention of finding a mate with the characteristics you esteem, and concentrate on how you will feel in the new relationship.

Timing Friday, waxing moon cycle or full moon

Candles Your astrological candle or other candle inscribed with your star sign, three pink tapers or small votive candles

Spell
My heart is open,
My love is on the way,
I rise up to greet him/her
As nature greets the day.

Incense Marjoram, rose, or honeysuckle

Crystals Rose quartz, aventurine

Oil Musk

Ritual Light the altar candle. Place the incense next to the altar candle and light it. Place the crystal near the altar candle. Anoint the astrological candle with the oil, working from the wick to the bottom, and place it in front of the altar candle. Anoint the three pink candles and place them in a triangular formation – one on each side of the astrological candle, and one in front of it.

Light the candles beginning with the astrological candle.

Chant the spell. Repeat the spell several times while gazing into the flames. Allow all of the candles to burn down completely.

Attracting a romantic relationship:

Timing Monday or Friday, waxing moon cycle

Candles Red seven-day candle, three small votive or straight candles one each in pink, white, and green

Incense Carnation or patchouli

Crystals Rose quartz and lapis lazuli

Herbs Rose petals or basil

Oil Amber, carnation, or gardenia

Spell

I now receive wholeheartedly the new love that is finding his/her way to me now. The rhythm of my heart now matches that of another. I am ready. He/She is here with me. Love is ours.

Ritual Light the altar candle and place the incense beside and light it. Place the herbs on the altar in a small dish or sprinkle them around the altar candle. Place the crystals in front of the altar candle. Anoint the red candle, working from the wick to the end. Place it on the altar. Anoint the green, white, and pink candles and place them in line in front of the red candle. Light the red candle, and then the green, white, and pink candles. Chant the spell. Look into the flames for several minutes while contemplating how you will greet your new love. Allow the candles to burn down.

Attracting a romantic relationship (2):

Timing Three consecutive Fridays, with the last Friday being just before or on the full moon.

Candles One large white pillar candle or three long white tapers; three pink votive candles

Incense Rose

Crystals Rose quartz and green apophyllite

Oil Amber for the white candle, and rose for the pink candles

Spell

A new love is mine, and his path is clear. With sure feet he comes to me as the universe illuminates his path. Closer, closer he draws to my warm embrace. I welcome my new love to my life.

Ritual On the first Friday, light the altar candle and incense, and carve your initials into the white pillar or into one of the white tapers. Anoint the white candle working from wick to end. Anoint one of the pink candles, and place them on the altar, about nine inches apart. Place the rose quartz near the white candle and the apophyllite near the pink candle. Light the candles. Chant your spell several times. If you are using a large pillar candle, snuff it out when the pink candle has burned completely down. If you are using a taper, allow it to burn all the way down. On the second Friday, light the altar candle and incense. Anoint the second pink candle and the second taper (or re-anoint the white pillar), and place them about six inches apart on the altar. Light the candles. Chant your spell several times, and allow the pink candle to burn all the way down. Repeat on the third Friday. This time, if you used a pillar candle, allow it to continue to burn all the way down.

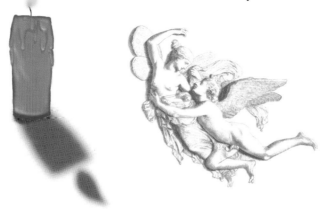

Reconciliation after a quarrel:

Use this ritual when the party you have quarreled with is not present and/or does not wish to take part in it. Use after quarrels between friends and siblings, as well as between married partners. You can use your own energies to encourage the reconciliation. Repeat the following week if necessary.

Timing Friday, waxing moon cycle or full moon

Spell

We emerge from the dark
All healed, to the light
Distance is banished
Closeness is nigh
Faith rediscovered
Is now within sight
We emerge from the dark
And healed, we face the light

Candles each in green, gold, and pink

Incense Apple or sandalwood

Crystals Lapis lazuli, amethyst, green tourmaline

Herb Yarrow root

Oil Rose

Ritual Light the altar candle. Place the incense near the altar candle and light it. Anoint the two green candles with the oil, working from the wicks to the ends. Place the green candles in front of the altar candle and place the crystals in front of them. Anoint the gold and pink candles, again working from the wicks to the ends. Place the gold candles in front of the green candles and the pink candles in front of the gold. Light the candles, beginning with the green candles. Light the herbs if you wish to burn some. Chant the spell.

Reconciliation (2):

This ritual is excellent when both parties wish to take part. It is best for reconciliation between lovers or mates.

Timing Friday, waxing or full moon

Candles Red figure candle depicting embracing lovers, preferably with two wicks, one from each of the figures' heads. One wick is acceptable if it is not from one of the figures' heads, but from a space between them.

Incense Ylang-ylang

Crystals Jade and emerald

Oil Rose

Herb Ginger

Spell

Anger and strife dwell with us no more. Forgiveness rules the day. Embracing we start anew. Our hearts pure and ready we begin again. Love reigns supreme in our dwelling, banishing hurt and resentment. Love, love, is our lot from here forward.

Ritual Light the altar candle and the incense. Carefully and slowly anoint the figure candle, working from wicks to end. If both parties are participating, each should anoint the candle in turn. Then place it in front of the altar candle. Light a small piece of charcoal, and place a tiny amount of dried ginger on the charcoal. Place the crystals near the figure candle, and light the candle. Chant the spell. If both parties are present, each should chant the spell in turn. Allow the figure candle to burn down completely. If it should go out before burning down, consider the ritual done, but incomplete, and repeat the following week with another candle. If the candle burns out leaving a shell of the embracing figures intact, the ritual can be considered finished and complete.

Fostering harmony and stopping arguments in a relationship:

Timing Tuesday, during the new or waning moon cycle

Candles Votive candles one black, one silver, and one indigo

Incense Lilac or lavender

Crystals Clear quartz crystal, green calcite

Oil Amber or lavender

Spell

As these candles banish disharmony and summon peace, so shall it be for all our days. As calm as a lake in morning, and as promising as a rainbow, our bond sways gently in life's breezes. Gently, gently we sway, harmony rules our days.

Ritual Light the altar candle and incense. Anoint the black candle from the end to the wick, and inscribe the names of both parties into the candle. Set the black candle in the center of the altar. Anoint the indigo and silver candles, working from wick to end, and set them one on each side of the black candle. Place the lapis at the base of the silver candle, and the clear crystal between the black and indigo candles. Light the black candle, then the blue and silver candles. Chant the spell. Allow the candles to burn down completely.

Strengthening a marriage:

Timing Friday, waxing moon cycle or full moon

Candles Use two altar candles, two red stick or taper candles, two small yellow votive candles, and two astral candles one for each of the marriage partners.

Incense Sandalwood

Crystals Opal, amethyst, and diamond

Oil Rose

Spell

My love and I are alternately root and tree, tree and root. We support and sustain one another and we each grow our own strong limbs. We face the future as two, and yet as one. We are each happy and powerful in our bond, giving and taking in like portion. Our commitment is strong, our lives joyful.

Ritual Place the two altar candles at the back corners of the altar and light them. Place the incense between the altar candles and light it. Anoint the two red candles, working from the wicks to the center, and then from the center to the bottom. Place the red candles in the center of the altar, slightly in front of the altar candles, with about six inches of space between them. Anoint the astral candles. If they are not already embossed with signs, carve your sign onto the bottom half of one of the astral candles, and that of your partner on the other. You may also carve your names if you wish. Set the astral candles in front of the red candles, about two inches apart. Anoint the yellow candles. Place them in front of the astral candles, about eight inches apart. Light the red candles, and chant your spell. Light the astral candles and repeat the spell. Light the yellow candles and repeat the spell once more.

Allow the candles to burn for a few minutes while you remain with them and concentrate on your desire. Keep the picture of your happy marriage firmly in mind. Next, extinguish the yellow and red candles. Allow the astral candles to continue to burn out completely.

Candle magic for physical healing

Recovery from serious illness:

Timing Saturday, waning moon cycle

Candles One black candle and an astrological candle representing the person who is ill. Be sure the black candle is not larger or thicker than the n candle.

Incense Frankincense, patchouli or sage

Crystals Plain quartz crystal, black onyx. You may add a crystal chosen according to the person's ailment if you wish.

Oil Patchouli

Spell

Banish ye illness
Banish ye weakness
Banish ye fear
Banish ye resignation
Healing and light are nigh!
On comes the light!
Illness does not abide the light
And so it retreats
Leaving strength and wholeness
Welcome ye strength and wholeness now!

Ritual Light the altar candle. Place the incense in front of the altar candle and light it. Holding the black candle, carve the sick person's name carefully into the wax. Underneath the name, carve the name of the disease he suffers from. Now anoint the black candle, working from the bottom end up to the wick. Place the black candle in front of the incense. Hold the astrological candle representing the ill person. Carve the patient's initials into the candle, and anoint it working from the wick to the end. Place the astrological candle next to the black candle so that they are touching. Place the crystals near the black candle.

Light the black candle, and then the astrological candle. Leave the candles until the black candle has burned out completely. When the black candle is burned out, extinguish the astrological candle.

Recovery from surgery:

Timing Tuesday, full or waxing moon

Candles One red figure candle or astrological candle for the recovering patient. One straight or votive candle in each of the following colors: green, orange, white, and red.

Incense Sandalwood

Crystals Carnelian

Herbs Pine

Oil Pine or lilac

Spell

As the universe is a perfect whole, so shall the body strive to become. The body has abilities and powers to heal itself, and these are being put into play now. The healing will be full and complete. Light surrounds the healthy body and glows from the site that is wounded no more.

Ritual Light the altar candle. Place the incense near the altar candle and light it. Hold the figure candle and find the place on it that corresponds to the location of the surgery. Mark the spot on the candle with a small nail or pin. Anoint the other candles from wick to end, and place them around the figure candle, one in each direction. Allow the colored candles to burn down completely. If the figure candle is still burning, light additional colored candles and repeat the spell. Allow the candles to burn down completely.

General health/healing:

Timing Sunday, waxing moon cycle

Candles One astrological candle for the person whose health is in question, one small light blue, and one small red candle

Incense Jasmine

Crystal Amber

Oil Gardenia

Herb Pine needles

Spell

The body seeks wholeness
It leans toward the light
Toward abundant strength and fullness
Toward vigor and might
The light enters, and disease flees!
The healing powers have won.

Ritual Light the altar candle and the incense. Etch the sick person's name into the astrological candle (their initials can suffice) and anoint it working from wick to end. Place it in front of the altar candle. Anoint the light blue and red candles and place them on either side of the astrological candle. First light the astrological, then the blue, then the red candle. Place the crystal near the astrological candle. Sprinkle pine needles on the altar. Chant the spell several times. Allow the candles to burn all the way down.

Relief of one's own pain:

Timing Sunday or Wednesday, waxing moon cycle.

Candles One votive candle in each of the following colors: red, white, green, and purple.

Incense Clove

Crystal Aventurine

Oil Juniper

Spell

I release my pain to whence it came
My body is healed, my strength restored
The message of pain was without blame,
Now relief of pain is my reward!
Lesson learned, I onward go Pain free, light as air,
in forward flow.

Herb Finely crushed barley

Ritual Light the altar candles and the incense. Anoint the red candle, working from wick to end, being sure to apply a good amount of oil to the base and sides of the candle. Dip or roll the candle in the crushed barley. (Only a small amount need affix itself to the candle). Place the red candle in the center of the altar. Anoint the white, green, and purple candles from wick to end, and place them in front of the red candle. Place the aventurine next to the red candle. Light the red candle, then the white, the green, and the purple. Chant the spell. Allow the candles to burn down completely.

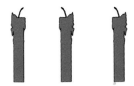

Relief of pain (for someone else):

Timing Sunday, Monday, or Wednesday

Candles Three red tea lights and one tall astrological candle representing the person who is in pain

Incense Clove

Crystal Aventurine

Oil Juniper

Herb Finely crushed barley

Other Picture of the person who is in pain. (The picture should depict the person when he or she is smiling and relaxed, and pain-free. If you do not have a photograph, a small drawing infused with your thoughts of the person can be substituted.)

Spell

White light surrounds, enters and fills.
Pain retreats, and will not return.
The light grows stronger, swirls and expands.
Pain is gone. Pain is gone.

Ritual Light the altar candle and the incense. Anoint the astrological candle, working from wick to end. Dip or roll the astrological candle in the barley, and place it in the center of the altar. Place the photo or drawing in front of the astrological candle. Place the aventurine in front of the picture. Anoint the red candle and place it in front of the crystal. Light the astrological candle, and then the red candle. Chant the spell several times, and allow the red candle to burn all the way down. Snuff out the astrological candle. Repeat the spell on the two following days, using a new red candle each time, and allowing the astrological candle to burn down completely on the last day.

Candle magic for attracting money and abundance

Money rituals should never be performed when you are feeling frustrated or upset about your situation. Try to release any fears you may have about not having enough. When you are vibrating fear, your magic will not be able to attract abundance, so it is vital that you relax your mind, focus on where you want to be when you have what you desire, and deflect your attention from the actual situation, if it is one of lack. Visualize yourself being able to pay the bills, getting a raise, giving to charity, or whatever your final goal may be, and feel the way you think you will feel when the desire is realized. Then you are ready to perform your ritual and bring what you desire to realization.

Gambling or investment luck:

Timing Thursday, full moon

Candles Orange, black, and white

Incense Rose

Crystals Peridot and agate

Spell
Money is making its way to me
I feel calm, sustained, and free.
Money quickly fills up my account
Feelings of gratitude abound.

Herb Mint

Oil Cinnamon

Ritual Light the altar candle and the incense. Anoint the black and orange candles, working from wick to end. Anoint the white candle and carve your initials or astrological sign into the bottom half of the candle. Place the candles on the altar in any formation you like, and place the crystal next to the white candle. Spread mint leaves around the altar. Light the white candle, then the black, and orange. Chant your spell several times and hold the vision of yourself winning or profiting from an investment. Then say, "I am grateful for what I have received!" Repeat this several times. Leave the candles to burn down completely.

Attracting fast money for a specific purpose:

If you are presented with an unexpected large bill, incur a sudden expense due to accident or illness, or need to help a child or friend and don't have the funds, this type of ritual can help attract a specific sum of money quickly.

Timing Sunday, full or waxing moon

Candles Astrological candle for the person in need of the money, and one brown, one gold, and one green candle

Incense Cinnamon

Crystals Garnet, aventurine, citrine

Spell

Money is making its way to me
I feel calm, sustained, and free.
Money quickly fills up my account
Feelings of gratitude abound.

Oil Jasmine

Other Small sheet of brown paper

Ritual Light the altar candle and incense. Anoint the brown candle, working from the wick to the end, and inscribe it with a dollar sign or the words "fast money." On the sheet of brown paper, write down the exact sum of money that will meet your immediate needs. Place the brown candle on the altar in front of the incense. Anoint the other candles from wick to end, and place your astrological candle very close to the brown candle, just behind it. Place the gold and green candles on either side of the astrological candle. Place your crystals in front of the candles. Light the candles. Chant your spell several times. Allow the candles to burn down completely.

Attracting prosperity and abundance:

Magic to attract prosperity will be more powerful if combined with a belief that you are worthy and deserving of abundance in life. Be sure your spell includes an affirmation that you deserve what you are asking for. If you do not feel that you do, your own vibrations of unworthiness will be counterproductive, and the magic will not be successful. Check your beliefs and try to align them with your desires before attempting the magic.

As you gain more prosperity, perform periodic rituals affirming this success and asking for its continuation.

Timing Thursday, full or waxing moon

Candles One green or white seven-day glass-encased candle and 28 orange votive candles. Use two large altar candles to anchor a strong energy.

Incense Bayberry

Crystals Malachite and citrine

Oil Bergamot

Spell
A deserving soul am I, and good!
All I wish comes to me and well it should.
Abundance and fortune will now be mine,
Prosperity is right for me, in space and time.

Ritual Light the altar candles at the back of each end of the altar. Anoint the exposed wax of the seven-day candle and place it in the center of the altar. Anoint the orange candles, working from the wick to the end, and place one on each side [E: Does this mean only two orange candles? See below] of the seven-day candle. Place the crystals among the candles. Light the seven-day candle, and then the orange candles. Chant the spell several times. Allow the orange candles to burn all the way down on the first day, while leaving the seven-day and altar candles lit. Each day for the seven days, light another four orange candles, and chant the spell several times. Allow the seven-day candle to burn down completely.

Attracting prosperity (2):

Timing – Thursday, waxing or full moon

Candles – Five green and one yellow votive candles; one astrological candle to represent the person who wishes for prosperity

Incense – Lavender or patchouli

Crystals – Citrine, malachite

Oil – Peppermint

Spell

Oh abundant universe, rich in all, send me what is mine! I attract a full portion. May I take part in the fullness of thy supply. Fortune now rains on me, and prosper I will! How grateful am I for the abundance that is mine!

Ritual – Light the altar candle and incense. Place the crystals in front of the altar candle. Anoint the astrological candle working from wick to end, and place it in front of the crystals. Anoint the green candles and place them in a line in front of the astrological candle. Anoint the yellow and candle and place it in front of the green candles. Light the candles, working from back to front. After the yellow candle is lit, chant the spell several times. Allow all of the candles to burn down completely.

Recalling loans or debts owed:

Before attempting to use magic to influence clients to pay what they owe you, or friends to repay a loan, be sure to let go of any anger you may have surrounding this debt. If you need to, use a magic ritual for the release of anger and animosity first. Incorporate into your spell the belief that from now on you will always be paid on time. Do not mention a specific person's name in your magic spell.

Timing – Saturday, during the full or waxing moon.

Candles – One yellow and one green

Incense – Jasmine

Crystals – Amber, topaz, emerald

Oil – Orange

Herbs – Nutmeg, honeysuckle

Other – Sheet of green paper, metal or glass bowl

Spell

I open myself to what is mine. I attract it unto me in timely manner Bring me what is mine, no less! As I have given, so I shall receive.

Ritual – Light the altar candle and the incense. Place the crystals at the front of the altar. On the sheet of green paper, write the amount owed to you if it is a specific debt you wish repaid. If you wish to initiate a general pattern of being paid in a timely manner by clients, write the statement: "My clients always pay me happily and on time. What they owe me will be paid quickly and soon." Place the paper on the altar, underneath one of the crystals. Anoint the candles, working from wick to end, and place them in the center of the altar. Light the candles, first the green and then the yellow. Take the sheet of paper, fold it several times, and using the flame of the green candle, set it on fire, and gently place it in the bowl. As it burns, chant your spell. Allow the candles to burn down completely.

Starting or building up a savings account:

Timing – Seven consecutive days during the waxing moon cycle, beginning or ending on a Thursday

Candles – Seven green straight or votive candles

Incense – Ginger

Crystals – Lodestone and citrine

Oil – Bergamot

Other – Several Chinese coins or coins of your country's currency

Spell

As the sapling grows into a tree, so my money takes root and flourishes. Each penny to a dollar grows and so it goes and goes and goes. As I decree so shall it be.

Ritual – Perform this ritual each day for seven days in a row. On each subsequent day, light the altar candle and incense, and place the lodestone and citrine in front of the incense burner. Anoint one of the green candles and place it in front of the crystals. Place the coins at the base of the candle, or under the lodestone. Light the green candle, and chant the spell several times. Allow the candle to burn down completely. Remove the coins and the other articles and begin each day with a clean and fresh altar. Repeat the ritual, using a new set of coins each day, adding them to the ones from the previous day(s). At the end of the seven days, place the lodestone and all of the coins used in the ritual in a box or drawer for several weeks.

Candle magic for success

New business:

Timing – Thursday, full or waxing moon

Candles – Two orange and one yellow candle, and the astrological candle for the person starting the new business

Incense – Clove

Crystals – Emerald and clear quartz

Oil – Bergamot

Other – (optional) A picture, a business card, or something else that represents the new venture.

Spell

My new business is in the right place and at the right time. It is beginning to prosper and succeed now. May these candles release a power that will attract my success to me! Strong and confident I march ahead, sure of my new venture. I am deserving, and success is mine.

Ritual – Light the altar candle and incense. Place any pictures or other objects on the altar. Anoint the astrological candle from wick to end, and place it in the center of the altar. Place the crystals on each side of the astrological candle. Anoint the other candles and place them in front of the crystals. Light the astrological candle, then the orange and yellow candles. Chant the spell in a loud and strong voice. Remain with the candles for a while, and then allow them to burn completely down.

Ongoing success in business:

Timing – Thursday, full or waxing moon

Candles – Votive candles – one brown, one green, one gold

Incense – Rosemary

Crystals – Citrine, amethyst, opal

Oil – Bergamot

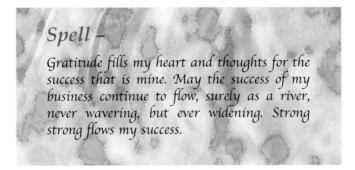

Spell –

Gratitude fills my heart and thoughts for the success that is mine. May the success of my business continue to flow, surely as a river, never wavering, but ever widening. Strong strong flows my success.

Ritual – Light two large altar candles, one in each back corner of the altar. Place the incense between the altar candles and light it. Place the crystals in front of the incense. Anoint the candles, working from wick to end, and set them in a line in front of the crystals. Light the candles, and chant the spell several times. Allow the candles to burn down completely. Repeat this ritual every few months during the proper moon cycle.

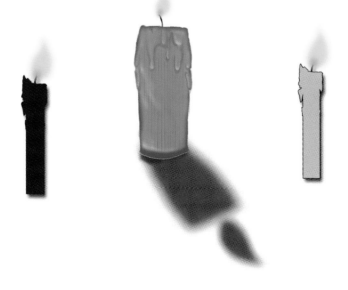

Finding a new job:

Timing – Thursday, full or waxing moon

Candles – One black taper, one gold votive, and one green votive

Incense – Peppermint

Crystals – Tiger's eye, lapis lazuli

Oils – Pine

Spell

Opportunity knocks and I answer gladly. The perfect job will now be mine. My employer awaits my arrival, and I meet the opportunity with joy. My new job is at hand this day!

Ritual – Light the altar candle and incense. Anoint the black candle, working from the wick to the end. Place the black candle on the left side of the altar. Anoint the green candle and place it in the center of the altar. Anoint the gold candle, and place it on the right side. Place the crystals between the green and black candle, and between the gold and black candle. Light the black candle, then the green, then the gold. Recite the spell. Concentrate on the feeling of having a new job. Leave the candles to burn out completely.

Passing an exam:

Timing – Waxing moon

Candles – One yellow and one orange

Incense – Musk

Crystals – Sodalite, aventurine, and tourmaline

Oil – Peppermint or violet

Spell

Sustain my intellect, protect my creative mind.
May I access my knowledge, and all in good time.
Success in my exam is assured, just as the flame
of the candle is pure.

Ritual Light the altar candle and incense. Anoint the yellow and orange candles, working from wick to end. As you work, picture a good grade on the exam and feel the relief it brings. Set the candles side by side on the altar and place the crystals in front of them. Light first the orange, and then the yellow candle. Chant the spell several times, each time with a stronger and more confident voice. Allow the candles to burn down completely.

Candle magic for personal growth

Gaining confidence and self-esteem:

Timing – Thursday, full or waxing moon

Candles – One tall yellow taper or other yellow candle, one silver votive and one purple votive (be sure the taper is large enough not to burn down before the votives; a small yellow pillar or other yellow candle can be substituted)

Incense – Carnation

Crystals – Hematite, red jasper, chalcedony

Oil – Ginger

Spell

My personal power knows no limit. I am a limitless being, deserving of all kindness, respect, and grace. Courageous I stand, knowing full well my worth and strength.

Ritual – Light two altar candles, and place the incense between them and light it. Anoint each of the candles, working from wick to end. Place the yellow taper in front of the incense, and place the red jasper near its base. Place the votive candles in front of the crystals, a few inches apart. Place the hematite next to the silver candle and the chalcedony next to the purple candle. Light the candles, first the yellow, then the silver and purple. Chant your spell, while picturing yourself in a situation where greater self-esteem will be of benefit to you. Picture your "ideal self" behaving and reacting in the situation. Chant your spell again. Allow the candles to burn down completely.

Being imbued with courage when facing adversity:

Timing – Saturday, full or waxing moon

Candles – One red, one orange, and one gold; votives or small straight or tapered candles may be used.

Incense – Musk

Crystals – Tiger's eye and aquamarine

Oil – Yarrow

Spell

My eyes are open
My steps are sure
Nothing shall deter me
My intentions are pure
Onward I march
Knowing not fear
My heart is courageous
The ring of victory I hear!

Ritual – Light the altar candle and the incense. Anoint the red candle working from wick to end, and place it in the center of the altar. Place one crystal on each side of the red candle. Anoint the orange and gold candles and place one in front of each of the crystals. Light the candles, beginning with the red, then the orange and gold. Chant the spell several times while envisioning yourself courageously facing your adversary or the situation in question. Maintain the visualization for several minutes. Allow the candles to burn down completely.

Developing creativity:

Timing – Wednesday, full or waxing moon

Candles – Straight candles, one each in yellow and orange

Incense – Lotus

Crystals – Chrysolite and chrysoprase

Oil – Peppermint

Spell

Ideas originate in my fertile mind. Joyously I bring them to fruition. I create with ease and joy, as the new and fresh come to me and through me.

Ritual – Light the altar candle and the incense. Anoint the yellow candle working from wick to end. Place it in the center of the altar, and place the chrysolite next to its base. Anoint the orange candle and place it next to the yellow one, with the chrysolite near its base. Light the candles. Chant the spell while nurturing a light and joyous emotion in your heart. Envision a white light surrounding the candles and your altar. Remain calm and serene, with an open feeling. Allow the candles to burn down completely.

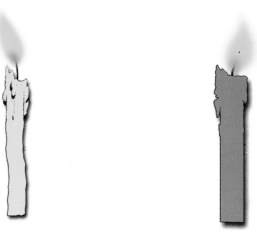

Breaking a bad habit:

In order to break a bad habit, two types of change have to occur. First, the habit must be banished or distanced from your range of desire. And second, in order to keep it at bay, a positive new behavior or thought process must replace the habit. It is advisable to perform two separate rituals. One will be a banishing ritual, and the other an acquisition ritual. It is vital that you be able to visualize yourself both without the bad habit and with the new behavior. Practice these visualizations for several days before attempting the magic rituals.

Be aware that you can not banish a habit from someone else, but only from yourself.

Timing – Tuesday, full or waning moon

Candles – One straight orange candle and one straight black candle

Incense – Cedar

Crystal – Jade

Oil – Clove

Herb – Rue

Other – Sheet of black paper and white paint or ink. Small charcoal block and heat-resistant bowl for burning the herb.

Spell

I hereby banish from my desire for/to _____. I see it retreat into the distance as a vague memory of my past. I was weak but now am strong. I was misguided and now am wise. I release my need and desire for _____ to the universe. There is no path for its return to me. I am grateful to be without it, and calmly move forward as it remains behind.

Ritual – Light the altar candle. Light the incense. Anoint the black candle, working from the end toward the wick. With a small nail or blade, inscribe the black candle with a symbol or word depicting the habit you wish to break.

Place the black candle in the center of the altar. On the black paper, use the white ink to inscribe the sentence: "I release my desire for/to _____." Fold the paper several times and place it under the black candle. Anoint the orange candle, working form the wick to the end, and place it to the left of the black candle. Place the jade crystal in front of the orange candle. Light the charcoal, and place a small amount of rue on it. Wait until it begins to smoke and spread the smoke around the altar.

Light the black candle, then the orange. Recite the spell while maintaining the vision of yourself banishing the bad habit and mentally forming a shield between you and the habit. Chant the spell eight more times. Leave the candles to burn down completely.

Candles

Light is considered to be the expression of divine energy, and candles are very important in wicca (as in many other religions). The candle is a symbol of enlightenment.

The color of the candles is very significant, and every color serves a different purpose in wicca.

White candles are the most useful ones. They are used in prayers and in initiation ceremonies. They symbolize pure light, cleanliness, and enlightenment.

A black candle can occasionally symbolize the goddess (together with a white candle that symbolizes the god).

Red or pink candles are used in rituals to solicit love, to send love, or to make contact with a beloved person who is far away. (Red candles stress physical passions; pink candles stress gentle love, softness and innocence.)

Green candles are used in rituals for Mother Earth and the animals and plants it contains. They are also used in rituals soliciting abundance and prosperity.

Brown candles are used when there is a need for a stabilizing effect. They are also used in rituals for healing Mother Earth and for linking up to it.

Blue candles are used in rituals for releasing self-expression and increasing creativity.

Purple candles are used for prayers and meditation whose objective is to reinforce extrasensory abilities. They can also be used for soothsaying.

Yellow candles are used for increasing joy, happiness, good fortune, and for requests for equilibrium.

Orange candles are used in rituals and prayers for increasing motivation and self-confidence.

Magenta candles are used for fortifying healing powers.

Breaking a bad habit (2):

Note that the previous ritual should be performed during the waning moon cycle, and this ritual should be performed as soon as possible afterwards, when the moon is begins to wax.

Before beginning this ritual, bear firmly in mind the new behavior or thought pattern with which you are replacing your bad habit. Be sure you feel happy and comfortable when performing the new action, so that you can visualize it strongly.

Timing – Thursday, waxing moon

Candles – Green, yellow, and white taper or straight candles

Incense – Rosemary

Crystals – Sodalite

Oil – Peppermint

Herbs – Dragon's blood

Other – Small charcoal block and heat resistant bowl for burning herbs.

Spell

I renew myself now and dedicate myself to change. With joy and strength I walk my new path. I become the new and the new becomes me.

Ritual – Light the altar candle and incense. Light the charcoal block and when it glows add a small amount of dragon's blood. When the herb begins to smoke, lift the bowl and pass the smoke around the altar. Place the bowl near the altar candle and allow the herb to finish burning. More can be added as it burns away. Anoint the green and yellow candles, working from wick to end. Place them side by side in front of the burning herb. Anoint the white candle, and place it, centered, in front of the other candles. Place the sodalite at the base of the white candle. Light the candles, first the green, then the yellow and white. Recite the spell several times, envisioning yourself having adopted the new behavior and feeling happy and relaxed. Allow the candles to burn down completely.

Attaining happiness:

Timing – Friday, full or waxing moon

Candles – One tall gold taper, one tall light blue taper, and one pink votive or short pillar candle

Incense – Gardenia

Crystal – Amethyst

Oil – Amber

Other – Several flower heads from pink, yellow and white flowers such as roses or carnations; a plate or a saucer

Spell

I make the choice, out loud, and clear
Only happy sounds I choose to hear
I make the choice, for it is right
Only to see the happy sights
I make the choice, with a nod and a wink
From now only happy thoughts shall I think.
For the choice IS mine, and I believe,
My world shall be AS I PERCEIVE!

Ritual – Light the altar candles and the incense. Anoint the gold taper from wick to end, and set it in front of the altar candle, slightly to the left. Anoint the light blue taper, and place it slightly to the right in front of the altar candle. Arrange the flower heads in a ring around the perimeter of the saucer. Anoint the pink candle, working from wick to end, and place it on the saucer, in the center of the flower heads. Place the saucer in the center of the altar, in front of the taper candles. Place the amethyst in front of the saucer. Light the gold candle, then the light blue, then the pink. Chant the spell three times, and allow the candles to burn down completely. (The pink candle should burn until the others have burned down. If it goes out before the tapers, light an additional pink candle and allow it too to burn down completely.)

Candle magic for consecration, memorial, and celebration

Remembering a deceased loved one (with more than one person participating):

This ritual can be performed on the loved one's birthday, on memorial days that are predetermined by your religion, or on holidays when the family is together and is acutely feeling the loss of the missing person.

Timing – Birthday of deceased, anniversary of death, religious memorial day or any other day when the loved ones of the deceased are gathered. Preferably but not necessarily during waxing moon cycle.

Candles – One white or purple glass-encased candle (can be seven-day candle if desired); one white straight or taper candle or white votive candle for each person taking part.

Incense – Patchouli or frankincense

Crystals – Two or more large clear quartz crystals with large points

Oil – Lotus

Other – Photo of deceased in which he or she appears alone, and another where he or she appears with one or more of the people present. The photos should be in frames that can stand on a table-top.

Spell

For this ritual you may chant a prayer for the dead that is particular to your religion, or read a passage that was meaningful to the deceased, or that appeals to the person leading the ritual. After this, chant the following:

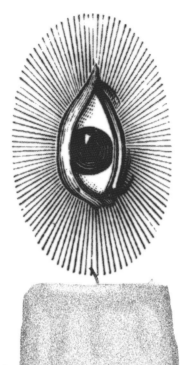

Safe in our hearts, and joined with our souls, your memory remains. You now travel in realms we have forgotten but will come to know again. With gratitude for what we gained by our bond with you in this world, we release you yet retain your memory with love. May your soul continue to grow and flourish.

Ritual – Light two large altar candles in each of the back corners of the altar. Light the incense and pass it among the participants. Place the incense between the altar candles. Anoint the exposed wax of the memorial candle, working in a clockwise direction, and place it in front of the incense, in the center of the altar. Place the crystals next to the memorial candle. Arrange the holders for the white candles around the memorial candle. Anoint the white candles one by one, working from the wick to the end. As each candle is anointed, hand it to one of the participants. Taking the last anointed white candle, light it in the flame of one of the altar candles. Light the memorial candle with the flame of your white candle. Say the first part of the spell (prayer or other portion) while holding your white candle. Now light each of the participants' candles in turn, beginning with the candles of children if there are any, from youngest to eldest. Each participant should place his own candle in a holder. When all of the white candles have been lit and placed, chant the second part of the spell. After a moment of silence, allow each participant to speak about the deceased and their positive memories, if they so wish. Allow the white candles to burn down completely. Extinguish the altar candles, and allow the memorial candle to burn down completely.

Celebrating the birth or adoption of a child:

Timing – Monday, full or waxing moon

Candles One straight or tapered candle in each of the following colors: white, gold, yellow, green, and pink; one straight candle in the child's zodiac color

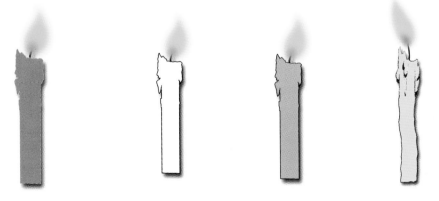

Spell

Welcome the new child to this realm of joy. May you proceed with your chosen lessons in this world with sureness of purpose and lightness of mind. May the pure light of happiness always shine upon you. May you always choose the path of goodness, strength, and prosperity. Love surrounds you this day, as evermore.

Incense – Rose or mint

Crystal – Rose quartz

Oil – The child's zodiac oil

Other – Small sheet of white paper and a pen with ink in the child's zodiac color.

Ritual – Light the altar candle and the incense. Anoint the straight candles working from wick to end, and place them in a straight line front of the incense, with the child's astrological candle on the far right, then the white, gold, yellow, green and pink candles. Write the child's full name on the sheet of paper, and fold it several times. Place the folded paper in front of the child's astrological candle, and place the crystal on the paper. Light the astrological candle, and then the other candles, from left to right. Chant the spell. Allow the candles to burn down completely.

Celebrating a wedding or wedding anniversary:

This ritual is for the couple to perform together, along with friends or family if desired.
Timing This ritual can be performed on the day before the wedding, and up to one week following the wedding. If it is an anniversary, perform the ritual on the anniversary itself.

Candles Two pink straight or tapered candles, one gold votive and one green votive

Crystals Rose quartz (large unpolished piece), and clear quartz crystal

Incense Frankincense

Oil Rose

Other Wedding rings or other gifts given each to the other. Small vase with twelve pink or white flowers, or small saucer with 12 pink or white flower heads arranged on it. White lace doily or other small decorative cloth.

White sheet of paper, and two pens, each with colored ink appropriate to the astrological sign of one of the partners.

Spell

Our love is a golden light that surrounds us, and a white light within us. Our love is healthy, and our love is strong. Our love is a bond yet we are not bound. Understanding guides our steps, and wisdom guides us to understanding. In rhythm with our higher selves we seek what life has to offer, and offer to it our best, individually and together. May we seek to be joyous individuals, and thus afford one another a clearer path to joy.

Ritual – Light the altar candle and the incense. Place the flowers in the center of the altar. Anoint the pink candles, working from the wick to the end, and place them side by side about a half-inch apart, behind the flowers. Place the rings or gifts on the doily in front of the flowers. Write the full names of the members of the couple on the white paper, each in his or her own astrological color. If the ritual takes place before the wedding and the bride will be changing her name, use the name she will be taking. Fold the paper once, and place it under the flowers. Place the quartz crystal to the right of the pink candle on your right, and the rose quartz to the left of the pink candle on your left. Anoint the green and gold votives working from wick to end, and place them in front of the gifts.

Light the pink candles, then the green and gold candles. Chant the spell. Allow the candles to burn down completely.

Consecration of a charm or talisman:

An object can never in and of itself provide us with "luck." We make our own reality and the events of our lives follow our train of thought. However, we can infuse and charge objects with our thoughts and vibrations, thus making them powerful "carriers" of our intentions and desires. An object thus charged, especially if the object itself carries some intrinsic meaning for its owner, can be used as a talisman, or "good luck charm." The talisman can be a piece of special jewelry, a watch, a crystal, or any other object which can be safely carried at all times and is a convenient size to keep in pocket or purse.

It is a good idea to be sure the talisman is waterproof and fairly durable. Use the following ritual to charge the talisman, in a similar manner to the programming of crystals discussed earlier.

Timing – Monday, full or waxing moon

Candles – One red and one black straight or votive candle

Incense – Lotus or frankincense

Crystals – Bloodstone and black obsidian or black onyx

Oil – Myrrh or lotus

Other – The object you wish to consecrate as a talisman

Spell

When you are near, I am protected. When you are near my aura is strong and bright. Keeping you near, I intensify my intention for joy and good fortune shall be mine. My steps will be wisely guided by my highest self, as long as you are in my possession. From this moment I consecrate you as my talisman.

Ritual – Light the altar candle and the incense. Anoint the black candle, working from the end to the wick while maintaining the intention to banish bad decision and blunders from your life. Anoint the red candle working from the end to the wick while maintaining the intention to bring joy and luck into your life.

Place the candles side by side in the center of the altar. Place the bloodstone and the onyx or obsidian in front of the candles, with the black stone near the black candle. Light the red and then the black candle. Hold the talisman and pass it back and forth slowly through the smoke of the incense. Chant the spell while doing this, and continue for a few more seconds, consciously infusing the talisman with your intentions. Place the talisman on the altar in front of the candles, and allow the candles to burn down completely. It is a good idea to re-consecrate your talisman at intervals, according to your intuition.

Expressing gratitude:

Giving thanks when things are going your way allows the universe to register that you would like it to continue in this manner! Taking time to perform this ritual will ground you in the joy of what you are grateful for, and assure that your thoughts remain focused on what you appreciate in life.

Timing – Monday, full or waxing moon is preferred. However, this ritual can be performed at any time and still be effective.

Candles – One straight or tapered candle in your astrological color; four small straight or votive candles – one silver, one gold, one pink, and one purple

Incense – Sage

Crystals – Clear quartz, rose quartz, and amethyst

Oil – Magnolia

Spell

For this ritual, use a spell you have written yourself, which simply states your thanks for whatever it is you are grateful for, or a general thanksgiving for the abundance of blessings in your life. Keep it simple, and hold the things, people, and feelings you are grateful for in your conscious thought as you recite your spell. End with "May my life continue to flow thus, in keeping with my highest good."

Ritual – Light the altar candle and the incense. Anoint the astrological candle working from wick to end, and carve your name into the top portion of the candle. Place it in the center of the altar, and place the crystals near its base. Anoint the small candles, from wick to end, and place them in a row in front of the astrological candle. Light the candles. Chant the spell several times, while gazing into the flame of the astrological candle, and then into the flame of each candle in turn. Allow the candles to burn down completely.

Candle magic for purification and protection

Protection from abuse (when you are the victim):

Timing – Tuesday, new or waning moon

Candles – Tall straight or taper candles, one each in black, white, and purple, and indigo

Incense – Patchouli

Crystals – Black obsidian, smoky quartz, and red jasper

Oil – Frankincense

Spell

When (abuser's name) approaches, my spirit expands.
My aura shines brightly, and repels all violence.
Peace reigns in my environs, now and always.

Ritual – Light two altar candles and place them in the back corners of the altar. Light the incense. Anoint the black candle, working from the wick to the end. Carve the abuser's name into the black candle and place it on the right side of the altar. Anoint the white and purple candles from end to wick, and carve your own name into the white candle. Place the white candle on the left side of the altar and the purple and indigo candles beside it, leaving as large a distance as possible between the black candle and the others. Place the red jasper near the white candle, and the black obsidian near the black candle. Place the smoky quartz near the purple candle. Light the purple candle, then the white, indigo and black candles. Chant the spell several times, and allow the candles to burn down completely.

Protection from enemies:

Timing – Waning moon, beginning on a Tuesday at least seven days before the new moon.

Candles – Seven candles in each of the following colors: purple, indigo, and magenta

Incense – Pine

Crystal – Aquamarine

Oil – Pine

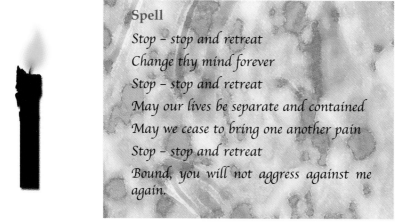

Spell

Stop – stop and retreat
Change thy mind forever
Stop – stop and retreat
May our lives be separate and contained
May we cease to bring one another pain
Stop – stop and retreat
Bound, you will not aggress against me again.

Ritual – Light the altar candle and incense. Carve the name of the enemy into the each of the purple candles. Anoint one candle of each color, working from wick to end. Place the anointed purple candle in the center of the altar with the anointed magenta candle on its right and the anointed indigo candle on its left. Light the purple candle, then the indigo and magenta candles. Chant the spell several times while looking into the flame of the purple candle. Visualize your enemy retreating and becoming smaller and smaller. Continue the visualization until your enemy "disappears." Allow the candles to burn out completely. Repeat the ritual each day at the same time, for a period of seven days.

Protection from gossip or slander:

Timing – Tuesday, waning moon

Candles – One black and white double action candle, with black on the bottom; one indigo straight or votive candle, and one black votive

Incense – Sandalwood or citronella

Crystals – Hematite and beryl

Oil – Lilac

Other – Small nail or metal pin

Spell

Words for ill shall not be spoke,
Words for good shall pour like smoke,
Only purely shall you speak,
Lies and slander no more shall be.

 Ritual – Light the altar candle and the incense. Anoint the double-action candle, working from the wick to the end. Stick the nail into the double-action candle where the black wax meets the white. Place the double-action candle in the center of your altar. Anoint the black votive candle from the end to the wick, and anoint the indigo candle from the wick to the end. Place the black candle to the left of the double-action candle and the indigo to the right. Place the stone at the base of the double-action candle. Light the candles and chant the spell several times. Allow the indigo and black candles to burn completely down. Allow the double-action candle to burn until it releases the nail. Then snuff it out and dispose of the remaining wax.

Purifying a home (space clearing):

Timing – Saturday, new or waning moon

Candles – One purple seven-knob or seven-day candle. Seven black, seven royal blue, and seven magenta straight or votive candles. Small white tea lights – on seven for each room in the home.

Incense – Myrrh or frankincense

Crystals – Bloodstone or clear quartz crystal

Herb - Basil

Oil – Yarrow or rose

Other – Flowers, holy water. (Holy water can be made by charging pure spring water with your intentions. Place your outstretched fingers over a bowl of water, and consciously charge the water with your desires and energy. When you feel the water flowing energy back to your fingers, the water is ready.)

> *Spell*
>
> *I fill this space with my loving energy. My home is empty of all predecessor energy, and ready for me to fill it with my presence and experiences. Light and love are welcome – dark spirits are banished.*
> *I proclaim this space pure and cleansed.*

Ritual – Light the altar candles and the incense. Place flowers in each room, and light a tea light next to each of the flower arrangements. Walk about the house with the incense, allowing it to infuse each room in turn. As you tour the house in this manner, keep thoughts of light and love flowing into the space, and banishing any negative or outside energies.

Returning to the altar, anoint the seven-knob candle, working from wick to end, and place it in the center of the altar. Anoint one black candle, working from the end to the wick. Anoint one royal blue and one magenta candle, working from wick to end. Place the black candle behind the seven-knob candle, and the magenta and royal blue candle on either side. Place the crystals near the base of the seven-knob candle. Light the seven-knob candle, then the other candles. Chant the spell. Carry the bowl of holy water to each room of the house in turn. In each room, gaze at the flame of the tea light, and chant the spell. Taking one of the flowers, dip its head into the holy water and sprinkle a small amount into the room. Allow the tea lights to burn down completely. Allow the seven-knob candle to burn just to the end of the first knob. The magenta and royal blue candles should burn down completely.

Repeat the ritual the next six nights, burning one knob of the seven-knob candle each night and using fresh magenta, black, and royal blue candles. Leave the flowers in the rooms of the home and light fresh tea lights each night as well.

Candle magic for termination or release

Release from negative behaviors or beliefs:

Timing – Tuesday or Saturday, new or waning moon

Candles – One black, one brown, and one white taper or votive

Incense – Cedar

Crystals – Hematite and smoky quartz

Oil – Pine

Other – Small photo of yourself in an envelope

Spell

I sense what is wrong
I know what is right
I turn from the wrong
I face toward the light

Ritual – Light the altar candle and the incense. Anoint the black candle, working from the end to the wick. Place the black candle in the center of your workspace, and your picture in front of it, in the envelope. Place the crystals on top of the envelope. Anoint the white and brown candles, working from the wicks to the ends, and place them on either side of the black candle. Light the black candle and recite the spell. Light the other candles, and chant the spell several times. Allow the candles to burn down completely.

Ending an unwanted relationship or friendship:

Sometimes we know that a certain lover or friend is no longer a positive influence in our lives, and that our relationship with this person is holding us back from growth. However, it is not always easy to end the relationship and release a person to whom we have become accustomed. This ritual will help with the process of accepting the ending and the subsequent release.

Timing – Tuesday or Saturday, new or waning moon

Candles – One votive or taper in each of the following colors: black, light blue, orange, magenta, and gray

Incense – Clove

Crystals – Lapis lazuli and snowy quartz

Oil – Juniper

Spell

I release my [relationship/friendship] with _____. As I have been nourished and as I have grown and as I have learned from him/her, so I now release him/her freely to the future. I open my hand, and wave our relationship goodbye with joy and gratitude. From this moment it is no longer part of my future, though it will be forever a part of my past. Change begins now. Release is complete.

Ritual – Light the altar candle and the incense. Anoint the black candle, working from the end to the wick. Place the black candle in the center of the workspace, and light it. Chant the spell while looking into the flame of the black candle. Anoint the other candles, working from the wicks to the ends. Place them in a line in front of the black candle, and light first the gray, then the other candles. Chant the spell several times until you feel something shift within you, indicating that you have accepted the release. Allow the candles to burn down completely.

Release from an unwanted suitor:

It sometimes happens that we are desired and pursued by a person in whom we have no interest. This unwanted pursuit can become irritating and sometimes even dangerous. If you have tried to turn the person down gently, to no avail, this ritual will help you remove the person – or at least his or her unwanted attentions – from your life.

Timing – Tuesday, new or waning moon

Candles – Two white or red figure candles, one representing your own gender and one representing the gender of the unwanted suitor. The figure candles should both be of the same color.

Incense – Rue or clove

Crystals – Agate, malachite, and smoky quartz

Oil – Juniper or patchouli

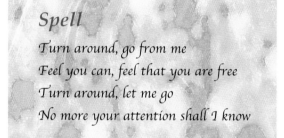

Spell

Turn around, go from me
Feel you can, feel that you are free
Turn around, let me go
No more your attention shall I know

Ritual – Light the altar candles and the incense. Anoint the candles working from wick to end, and carve your initials into the candle representing your gender. Carve the suitor's initials into the other candle. Set the candles in the center of the workspace, back to back, about one inch from one another. Place the crystals in the space between the candles. Light the candles, and chant the spell three times. Allow the candles to burn for one hour, and snuff them out. Each subsequent day, move the candles one or two inches further apart, light them, chant the spell three times, and allow the candles to burn for one hour. The number of days you continue the ritual will depend on the size of the figure candles.

Release from a hex, curse, or "evil eye":

Timing – Saturday, new or waning moon

Candles – One black seven-knob candle and seven votives in each of the following colors: royal blue, silver or gray, magenta, and purple

Incense – Cedar

Crystals – Black onyx, black obsidian, sardonyx, and clear quartz crystal

Oil – Patchouli

Other – Photo of yourself or the person under the influence of the curse

Spell

I call upon all the forces of good, all of my guides, my angels, and my own higher powers, to converge upon this negative energy and return it to whence it originates. Send it away from me with a powerful reversal and release. May I be purified and free, and protected from its evil for all my days. I immerse myself in white light and facilitate this release.

Ritual – Light two altar candles, and place the incense between the altar candles and light it. Anoint the black seven-knob candle, from the end to the wick. Place the photo and the black candle in the center of the altar and light the black candle. Place the crystals near the base of the candle, or on the photo. Anoint one of each of the other colored candles, working from the wicks to the ends, and place them in front of the black candle, in a row from left to right. Light the candles. Chant the spell. Replace "I" with the name of the hexed person if you are performing this ritual for someone else. Allow the colored candles to burn down completely, and snuff out the black candle after one knob has burned. Repeat the ritual for the next six days, preferably at the stroke of midnight.

The rose of love

The man yearns for the young woman, the woman yearns for the handsome young man - what do they do? How do they fulfill their love?

Among many European nations - the Italians, the Romanians, the Greeks, and the Gypsies - we find a spell in which the rose, preferably a red one, is used for this purpose.

This is what the amorous man - or woman - has to do:

1. Select a fresh, half-open red rose. If you pluck the rose from the bush with your own hands, do it at sunset. (In an ancient book of Greek origin, there is an additional warning: if the lover is pricked by the thorns of the rose, and a drop of blood falls on the ground, he should throw the rose to the ground and wait eight days before repeating the procedure. So, dear readers and lovers of spells, be careful of thorns!)

2. Purchase or prepare three tall, red candles. (If you use candles scented with aromatic fragrances, you should go for a jasmine-scented candle.)

3. Before going to sleep, place the rose in a glass of water or a vase next to your bed. With the three candles, create a triangle around the glass or vase containing the rose.

4. Go to sleep... and try to dream about your beloved the whole night.

5. At dawn - it's very important that you do this before the sun rises - position the rose so that it is facing east to greet the rising sun. You must stick the stem of the rose into a pile of sand in a glass or an empty jar, or in a flowerpot filled with sand. The rose can be placed on the windowsill, the roof, or in the yard.

6. Now take two of the red candles from the triangle surrounding the rose, stand them on either side of the rose, and light them.

7. While the candles are burning, think about your beloved in your heart and say aloud: "This red rose is the messenger of true love. These candles will convey my love to my beloved's heart..." and think about his/her name without saying it aloud.

8. Now return the rose to its place next to your bed (not in a glass or vase containing water) and (carefully!) put the burning candles in next to it. Let the candles burn down.

9. Leave the rose and the remains of the candles (the wax) in the same place for three days and three nights.

10. On the morning of the fourth day, take the withered rose petals, the remnants of wax from the burnt-down candles, and the third, whole, candle. Place all of this in a cloth or red paper bag.

11. Bury the bag in a hole you have dug in the ground, and cover the hole well.

12. And now, all you have to do is to go and phone or send a letter or e-mail to the person on whose behalf you have gone to so much trouble.

Candle magic for spiritual growth

Communication with the spiritual realm:

It is a good idea to meditate for a while before beginning this ritual.

Timing – Monday, full or waxing moon

Candles – Tall taper candles – one white, one purple

Incense – Lotus

Crystals – Amethyst, celestite, and apophyllite

Oil – Myrrh

Spell

I rise upward in consciousness to meet whomever may choose to communicate with me. I exist beyond my physical sense, ready to know whatever message is there for me. I am open. I am ready. May I know the spirit realm, and may it blend with my consciousness.

Ritual – Light the altar candles and the incense. Anoint the candles, working from wick to end. Place the candles side by side in the center of the altar and light them. Place the crystals on the altar at the base of the candles. Light the candles, and chant the spell several times. Close your eyes and speak whatever may come into your mind in addition to the spell. Remain quiet and open, and stay near the altar until the candles have burned down an inch. If you do not feel contact has yet been made, leave the altar, but remain open to any signs or feelings you may experience in the next few hours. Allow the candles to burn down completely.

Candle divination

Until now we have explored candle magic for the realization of desires or change. We have used the energy of the candle to try to bring about particular outcomes in the material world. Divination or "fortune-telling" is another powerful use of candle magic. Almost everyone has wished to be able to look into the future, and with a bit of skill, even a novice can use candle magic to accomplish this. All that is needed is a basic knowledge of interpretation of the flames and/or the melted wax, along with a powerful focus of mind. The candle will focus your energies and allow your own psychic powers to help you see the future and divine truths from the present. You will open up your already existent ability to connect with the psychic realm.

Divination with candles can be performed for three major purposes:

- Ascertaining truth
- Decision-making
- Seeing future events

This type of magic does not entail the manipulation of external events or petitioning the universe for something to happen. Instead, it asks the universe or our higher selves for knowledge and communication. The candle or other divination tool is used as a conduit to knowledge about the present and future, which we would not otherwise have access to with our conscious minds. It is believed that all knowledge – past, present, and future – exists as thought energy in the universe, and is available to all of us. Divination is a way to bring to conscious knowledge that which is already known in the vast realm of universal wisdom.

Keep in mind that the future is not prescribed! Whatever you may learn from divination is a potential future, according to the path being followed at the time you perform the ritual. Change the path – and you change the future! Your thoughts, decisions, and actions are what will ultimately make your future happen. The information you divine from candle magic can be used as input to help you think, decide, and act in accordance with your hopes and dreams being realized. Whatever you see is still open to your conscious abilities to change it. If you are given a vision of the future which is unappealing to you, know that you have the power to use that information to fashion a different outcome. Divination will show you possibilities. Use them as guidance and counsel, not as foregone facts and conclusions.

Divination is dependent on your openness to the messages you will receive. You must be sure before beginning that you have no vested interest in learning a particular thing, or being shown a particular outcome. A profound openness is vital to the success and veracity of the divination. With petition magic, you concentrated on communicating through the magic in order to affect something that was happening. With divination, however, you must be open to communication coming to you, rather than try to send it out. You must not try to will the candle to behave in a particular way or to show you a particular answer or outcome.

Often human beings are not certain of their perceptions of reality. We can wonder if the way we see things is the actual truth, and we are sometimes in a dilemma over which possible interpretation of a situation we should accept as our truth. Truth, of course, is dependent upon the beholder, and it should always be born in mind that in seeking it, we seek our own individual truth, as opposed to an absolute truth.

Ascertaining truth and decision making is done by asking a question and obtaining the answer from the candle flame or wax. The formation of the question is of utmost importance. Questions are of two types – open and closed.

An open question is a question that cannot be answered with a word or phrase. It is answered sometimes with an entirely new question, or with suggestions leading to other, perhaps as yet unthought of ideas. An open question can be answered with information, but never with a definitive short answer. Examples of open questions are:

- "What new opportunities lie before me this year?"
- "How can I help my son have better self-esteem?"
- "What should I consider when choosing a new home?"

Before setting out a candle in hopes of receiving answers to an open question, be sure you are open to any and all answers you might receive. In this case, try not to visualize a particular action on your part. Don't visualize helping your son with homework, for example. Instead, hold your real goal in mind – a son with high self-esteem. You might picture him happy and smiling and surrounded by friends. Leave out your own role or actions – those are what you are asking for guidance for. Be open to that guidance.

If you are asking for guidance in choosing a new home, picture yourself happily moving and packing, and be open to guidance as to where and how you should approach your search. An open question will respond best to an open asker!

Closed questions are those that can be answered "yes" or "no" or with a definitive short answer such as a choice between two options. Examples of closed questions are:

- "Shall I quit my job?"
- "Is my present boyfriend the man I should marry?"
- "Is this a good year to make a move to a new home?"

When asking this type of question, you should bear in mind that the candle ritual will rarely give you a short and definitive answer. More often you will be guided to look at aspects of the situation that you may not have considered and that will help you answer your question yourself. You can ask the candle to show you "yes" or "no," but be sure that this type of question is most beneficial to you before you begin.

When you use candle divination for decision-making, try to think carefully beforehand of the most appropriate alternatives. Project yourself into each one of the possibilities and visualize yourself already having made the decision. Ask yourself how you feel. Is there one alternative that makes you feel physically stressed or even ill? Is there one that makes you feel anxious? Try to eliminate any possible decisions that clearly give you negative feelings at the outset. When you have narrowed the field down to two or three alternatives, it is time to infuse the candles with those, and to perform a ritual.

Fortune-telling, like ascertaining truth and decision-making, begins with a question. Try to make the question as open as you can. Rather than "Will I be married in five years?" ask "What should I look for in a mate?" Be sure within yourself that you are open and receptive to whatever comes up during the divination session.

Candle colors for divination

As with magic for petition, divination will be more powerful if you match your candle to the question you are asking. In general, straight or tapered candles that are not too thick or tall are best for divination. White can be used for any question and can be considered an all-purpose color.

Green: For questions having to do with new beginnings, money and prosperity, abundance, and births or children

Blue: For questions about healing, illness and disease, and recovery from pain and sickness.

Pink: For questions having to do with relationships with friends

Red: For questions about love, sex, and romantic relationships

Purple: For questions dealing with psychic phenomena, and power and authority in dealings with others

Black: For questions dealing with changing of luck

Orange: For questions about physical activities and mental powers

Yellow: For questions about relocation of home or business, and for seeing into the future.

Before you begin:

Once you are certain that you have formulated the appropriate question for your divination, choose a time to perform your ritual when you will not be disturbed. Keep in mind that unlike petition magic, you will want to remain near the candle until you have your answer, and you will not simply leave the candle to burn down, in most cases. You will need to observe the burning of the candle carefully in order to ascertain your answer.

It is not necessary to burn altar candles and incense for a divination ritual, but it is advisable. The altar will help focus your energies and get you into the right frame of mind. It is a good idea to write down your question, and bring it to the altar on a folded piece of paper. Use an oil appropriate to the type of question you are asking and carefully anoint your candle. When you are ready to begin, be sure to concentrate your thoughts and try to maintain your concentration throughout.

Divination with one candle:

For open questions, after you have lit the candle, observe it carefully, and simultaneously observe your own feelings and emotions as the candle burns. Together these will impart information to you.

If the flame is strong and reaches up high, the candle is attuned to your energy and communicating strongly. If the flame leaps and jumps, however, it may be picking up some indecisiveness on your part. A leaping flame may also mean that your emotions surrounding the question you have posed are not stable.

Try to bring yourself into focus with your question, and see if the flame responds. If it continues to burn in an erratic manner, perhaps it is not a good time for you to ask this question, and you'd best try another day.

A very small or weak flame might also indicate that the energies are not strong enough for you to perform this ritual at this time. It may also indicate that you have not communicated your desire or question strongly enough. When the flame seems to twist itself into a spiral, this is a warning of imminent danger.

If the candle makes muted popping and cracking sounds, there may be a message for you. Try to quietly listen and observe and be alert to what you are feeling. The message will become clear if you remain focused.

If the candle makes loud popping sounds, it is having to deal with negative forces and thoughts.

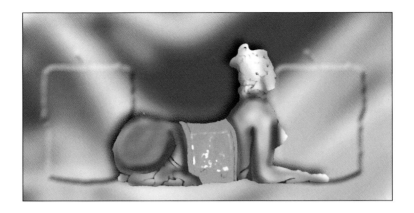

Sometimes smoke will rise from the candle, and this too can help in interpreting the divination. When the smoke from the flame rises to the north, something is manifesting in the physical realm. This may indicate a need for you to engage in some type of physical activity or labor. If you have asked a question concerning your health, north-pointing smoke may mean you should see a doctor for a checkup, or seek medical advice. It may also mean your finances need taking care of.

When the smoke rises in a southerly direction, you are getting a positive sign from the candle. For health questions, this can mean you are on the mend, and for questions of relationships it can mean a new love is on its way, or that your relationship is improving. Whatever the question, if the smoke heads south, you are getting an auspicious answer.

If the smoke from the candle rises to the east, you need to devote some thought to your situation. Some mental calculation and logic is in order. The candle is telling you to "use your head" and think things through.

When the smoke rises to the west, you are being ruled by uncontrolled emotions. Your feelings surrounding the question are quite intense and are directing your actions. A cooling-off period could be in order before moving forward on this issue.

For yes/no questions, watch the candle carefully. In general, a strong bright flame, especially with smoke reaching toward the south, means "yes," whereas a weak flame that threatens to go out means "no." However, you can choose in advance what indicates "yes" and what indicates "no," and communicate this to the candle before asking your question. Then interpret accordingly. It is possible to assign one side of the candle to "yes" and the other to "no." The side of the candle that burns down faster is your answer. Another method is to notice which way the flame leans. A flame that leans toward you means the answer is "yes," and away from you means "no."

If the flame goes out prematurely, your question may be inappropriate, or the timing is wrong.

Divination with two candles:

For closed questions with two alternatives such as yes or no, it is possible to set out two candles and decide that the candle that burns out first is the one that gave you its answer. Alternatively, the one that continues burning is the answer!
Assign one candle to mean "no" and one mean "yes."

Communicate this choice while anointing the candles. Light the candles, and concentrate on your question without willing the candles in any way.

Two candles can also be used to choose between two alternatives. Anoint each candle with one of the possibilities in mind, light the candles, and the one that burns down more quickly is the answer.

Divination with three or more candles:

For questions about the future, choose three white candles of the same size, and set them in a triangular formation on the altar. Four candles can be used as well, with three in a triangular formation and the fourth placed in the center of the triangle. Light each candle, stating your question as you light each one in turn. Think about your question as you watch the flames.

Some possible interpretations include:

If one of the candles goes out suddenly, long before the others, disaster is imminent.

A flame moving from side to side means that there is travel in your near future.

One of the candles burning noticeably brighter than the others portends success and good fortune.

Sparks flying up from a flame means caution is necessary.

A rising and falling flame is a warning that danger is approaching.

A glowing wick means good luck.

If a wick leans to one side, change is in the offing.

When one candle burns dimly, something may be about to go wrong in one of your relationships. This could also mean that some plans you have made will not come to pass.

D i v i n a t i o n   w i t h   w a x :

When asking a closed question, use one candle and watch carefully as the wax begins to drip down the sides. If the wax drips only to the left, the answer is no. If it drips to the right, the answer is yes.

Some candles burn down to a "puddle" of wax. The shapes you see in this wax can tell you something about your question. Be open and use your intuition. Write down the shapes you see. They may not make sense to you immediately, but later will give you important clues and information.

Another way to divine with wax is called ceromancy. This is the art of interpreting the wax formations achieved from dripping melted wax directly from the candle into a bowl of water.

Using a dark bowl filled with cool water, light a candle, and hold it tilted over the bowl as it burns. As the wax drips into the water it will harden into formations. Watch carefully, and the moment a discernable image comes into view, stop dripping the wax, and make note of the image you received. It may be a picture, a symbol, or letters or numbers. Think carefully about what this image may mean for you and the question you have asked. Interpretation is very personal, and a symbol that means one thing to you can mean something vastly different to someone else. Your first thought in relation to the shape you see is the most significant. The following are a few traditional interpretations of wax formations. Your own interpretations of the same symbols may differ.

Acrobat An acrobat, in the form of a tumbler or gymnast, always symbolizes a love affair, especially if the seeker is a woman. In the case of a man, the interpretation would be a love affair involving a woman connected to him.

Angle This formation is always interpreted as a better future awaiting the seeker. In the case of a sick person, or someone who is worn down physically or emotionally, an angel is a sign that "somebody up there is watching over him." The figure of an angel is highly significant for infertile women: it assures them that they will bear a child.

Ant The figure of an ant, or many ants in a row, reflects the well-known saying from the Book of Proverbs: "Look to the ant, lazy one; consider its ways and learn from them." The precise interpretation is: Diligence and perseverance will pay off in the end!

Antler The antlers of a deer or similar animal are an unmistakable sign of infidelity, sexual problems, quarrels between a husband and wife, and the like.

Apple Indicates great achievements for the seeker. A partly eaten, or damaged, apple lessens the formation's importance.

Arrow Bad news.

Avocado The avocado indicates positive developments within the individual's close family circle.

Axe Many difficulties. The person will be able to overcome his problems, but it will take a lot of work.

Baby A formation that indicates a generation gap, but doesn't show in which direction.

Back A formation that presents the back of a person, generally without a clearly discernible head, indicates that the seeker is unsure of his way in life. It seems that there is another person - on whom he is dependent, or whose path he is following - who is charting a course for him without bringing the seeker into the decision-making process.

Ball A ball generally denotes upheaval in the seeker's life, movement from one situation to another, from one position to another, changing fortunes.

Balloon A balloon signifies minor, fleeting problems that do not leave much of a mark on the person. Your problems are about to be eased.

Banana The banana, due to its suggestive shape, is always associated with sex. In most cases, it is interpreted as infidelity or a significant problem (especially if the seeker is a male). A peeled banana indicates that the problem is getting worse.

Barrel A barrel indicates great wealth, whereas a broken or open barrel signifies a loss of riches.   A barrel can also be interpreted sexually, as a sign of virginity in both men and women. An intact barrel means complete virginity; a broken barrel indicates past sexual experience.

Basket A present awaits the seeker, or a gift that he received in the past had a practical worth far greater than its monetary value.

Bat A significant formation. It indicates that the seeker is well-schooled in disappointment, and is constantly fearful that people - even close friends - are constantly plotting against him.

Bathtub A shape that indicates flirtations - brief, fleeting love affairs.

Beach This formation indicates that the seeker is under great pressure; in fact, it is a clear call for help.

Bead A bead, which is distinguished mainly by the hole in its center, is sometimes interpreted as a sign of children. One bead signifies one child; two beads, two children, and so on. Beads can also be interpreted as troubles which await the seeker - troubles that he is capable of overcoming.

Bear Separation. A long trip, or a constraint of some sort, will take the seeker away from his family and his surroundings for a lengthy period.

Bed Always a sign that the seeker hides his feelings and problems behind a "mask" of indifference. There is no special connection to sexual problems.

Bee Financial success on a large scale awaits the seeker. His riches will gain him fame and glory on the social front. Always a good sign. For a woman, it can suggest marriage to a wealthy man. The interpretation remains the same whether we see a single bee or a swarm.

Beehive As with a single bee, a beehive indicates success in business. The greater the number of bees around the hive, the greater the success. Note that a broken, abandoned or smashed beehive signifies a serious business failure.

Beetle A serious scandal threatens, or has threatened, the seeker. The scandal will obviously be a decisive factor in his life.

Beggar A formation that signifies financial strain or a fear of poverty. At times, it may indicate problems in functioning brought on by these fears.

Bell Surprise! Unexpected news will change your life!

Belt A formation that indicates strong self-discipline. The seeker is capable of taking matters in hand and achieving his objectives.

Bicycle Relations with a close partner are highly significant.

Bird A bird or birds always indicate good news for the person.

Boat A boat indicates that an important change has taken place, or will take place, in the life of the seeker as a result of someone's visit to him, or his visit to a different locale.

Book A book symbolizes trials or struggles that the seeker must undergo. The basic interpretation depends on the state of the book: a closed book indicates difficult "tests" on a daily basis (in the past or future), whereas an open book means that the person is successfully withstanding his trials and will continue to do so. If the specific book can be identified (Bible, dictionary, cookbook, and so on), the interpretation is based on the subject of the book.

Boomerang A boomerang is the classic symbol of betrayal, or an enemy who is just waiting for the chance to stab the seeker in the back. The betrayal is not necessarily sexual in nature; it can take the form of someone tattling to the income tax authorities, for example.

Boot The road to achievement is open to the seeker; he has only to take the first step!

Bottle A complex shape. It indicates, first of all, health problems that endanger the individual. It can signify addiction to a substance or pastime, such as gambling, and can also point to sexual problems.

Bouquet This is a sign of great honor and important achievements... but also of death!

Bow A bow, with or without an arrow, suggests a love affair which revealed the uglier sides of the seeker's character - nasty gossip, wrongful treatment of the partner, etc.

Box Problems in the romantic sphere. If the lid is open, the problems will be solved. It is difficult to distinguish between a box, a package, a jar, and so on.

Bracelet The seeker is "bound" to his beloved!

Bread Whenever a loaf of bread appears, the interpretation will lean towards the material realm.

Breast The clearly-defined shape of a breast or breasts indicates a close connection between the seeker and his mother - to the point of over dependence!

Brick A brick or bricks symbolize the seeker's creativity and ability to bring his desires to fruition, not necessarily in the material realm. Bricks in any form - as a single brick, a pile or a wall - indicate a positive interpretation.

Bride A formation containing the figure of a bride, points us toward our interpretation: in the eyes of the seeker (male or female), a "formalized" love relationship is of paramount importance, but there are obstacles along the way to this much-desired goal.

Bridge An important formation. First of all, a bridge symbolizes the seeker's search for divine truth, for a link with his God. A bridge also indicates difficulty in forging a meaningful connection with a partner.

Broken ring Divorce or separation

Bubble This formation is interpreted as a feeling of pressure or strangulation experienced by the seeker.

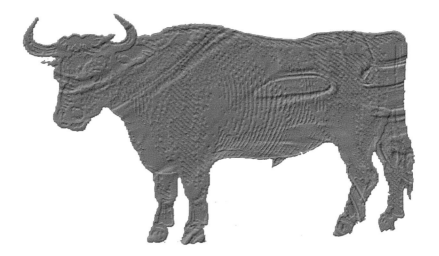

Bull Argumentative tendencies. The person must curb his anger!

Bush A bush indicates that new horizons are opening up for the seeker.

Butterfly Capriciousness, a certain degree of hypocrisy - but not in extreme form. Numerous sexual experiences. Important: this formation indicates that the seeker stretches - but does not cross - the boundaries of good taste.

Button A person close to the seeker is hiding important matters or information from him. Keep your eyes open!

Cage A cage, especially a bird cage, indicates obstacles and difficulties that seriously hamper the seeker. When the door of the cage is closed, these problems cannot be solved immediately; when it is open, the problems can be solved, with great effort. If the door of the cage is closed, and we see a figure inside the cage, the situation is very serious!

Camel In principle, a camel is a "good" formation - a sign that there will be a change for the better in the person's life.

Camera Indicates that his outward image, or "what people think of me," is the most important factor in the eyes of the seeker.

Candle A happy marriage to which the seeker is in some way connected - whether as a member of the couple, their child, or a parent of either spouse. The candle also carries a strong mystical significance, generally representing the desire to expand one's knowledge in a religious, mystical direction.

Cannon Congratulations! Good news! Things that were not possible in the past are becoming a reality today. Troubles will be solved!

Car A formation which indicates that the seeker is truly cut off from reality.

Carpet Danger! Someone is just waiting to "pull the rug out" from under the seeker.

Carrot Contrary to first impressions, a carrot is not a formation that symbolizes sexuality; rather, it suggests a cowardly nature. In the case of a man, we can also add that he is unwilling to take responsibility for himself.

Castle Financial success will come to the seeker not as a result of his own deeds, but through an inheritance, the actions of someone close to him, or marriage with someone wealthy.

Cat Unkind people are talking behind your back. Untrustworthy people are about.

Cat A cat is a significant figure. Betrayal, disloyalty. This formation warns the seeker of betrayal and treachery, but does not indicate its source.

Chain A chain takes its true interpretation from what surrounds it. As a positive sign, it points to a solid marriage; if negative, it indicates subjugation to someone.

Chair An unexpected visit by a close friend, or a "true love" from the past, will change the course of the seeker's life.

Check A bank check indicates that the seeker's statements should be weighed carefully; every check is presumed to be "made of rubber"!

Cherry One or more cherries (usually a pair) always relate to a love affair.

Chest Generally appears in the form of a woman's breasts, but can also be man's chest. In any event, this formation signifies the pursuit of true love (not necessarily sexual in nature). In women, it can also indicate the desire to have a child.

Child The figure of a boy or girl indicates that the seeker places great importance on family ties.

Chimney A chimney on the roof of a house signifies hidden dangers lying in wait for the seeker. Smoke rising from the chimney intensifies the sense of danger.

Chrysanthemum Always a good sign. This "sun flower" will always fortify the seeker, especially if he is a young man.

Cigar New friends are "redesigning" the seeker's life in an unknown direction.

Circle Your problem will be resolved.

Circle A circle, which sometimes appears in the form of a ring, relates to the area of love or marriage. An intact circle symbolizes romantic success, marriage, reconciliation with a romantic partner, and the like. A broken circle signifies problems in these same areas. A circle with a small hill in the center (resembling a breast viewed from above) means that the birth of a child will affect the seeker.

Clock Always a good sign! It means that the person will progress in life over the course of time; matters will now move forward in a positive direction. An hourglass tells the seeker that he should dare to do what he truly wants. A sundial indicates that the person should act on his decisions, and assures him of success in all his endeavors.

Closet A figure of a closet indicates that the seeker possesses strong spiritual powers, and perhaps has extra-sensory perception (i.e. skills as a medium).

Clothing A formation that resembles clothing in general indicates that the seeker is an incorrigible egotist who focuses primarily on himself.

Cloud A cloud or clouds carry a harsh meaning, i.e., disaster! Look to the other signs for a clue to the nature of the catastrophe, and advise the seeker to try to overcome it.

Clown A clown formation signifies a party or other social event that is likely to affect the seeker's life - if it hasn't already done so.

Coat A friendship or partnership is about to end.

Coffin Knock wood! This is a formation that foretells the worst kind of bad luck.

Comb The seeker was involved, in one way or another, in a major act of fraud or deceit.

Comet A unique formation, difficult to distinguish. It consists of a star trailing "sparks" in its wake. A comet indicates an unexpected guest who can bring about a total change in the life of the seeker.

Conch Shell A conch or other sea shell tells the seeker that he must "keep his ears open," i.e., listen to what's going on around him. We can predict that he will hear good news in the near future.

Corpse Knock wood! This is a message from "the great beyond" that you will shortly find yourself in just such a sad state!

Crocodile Beware! Do not hurt others, because next time you may be on the receiving end.

Cross A cross is a good sign, primarily with regard to health.

Crown You or someone else near you will become ill.

Crown A significant formation. A tendency to engage in the supernatural and mysterious. There is nothing wrong in this; let your natural leanings determine your areas of interest.

Cubes of Dice Cubes have meaning only if they appear as (at least) a pair: a strong tendency to gamble (with a good chance of losing "big"!).

Curtain A curtain or screen indicates that someone close to the seeker is hiding important things from him. More is concealed than is revealed!

Dagger A dagger, which is distinguished from a knife by its curved blade, signifies danger. Someone close to the seeker will stab him in the back!

Daisy A flower which is difficult to identify. It indicates a new love, or the flowering of an old one.

Deer In the coffee grounds of a man:

A quarrel or dispute with someone close to him is bothering the seeker. The right thing to do is bring the subject of the quarrel out into the open and solve the problem, because the relationship with this person is more important than whatever caused the fight in the first place. The deer's antlers indicate the area of disagreement.

Detective The shape of a detective, for example the profile of Sherlock Holmes which is easily identifiable, signifies insecurity, a suspicious nature, nosiness, and mistrust in relationships with friends and even family.

Devil The figure of a devil suggests a leaning towards exploration of the unknown, coupled with a fear of what lies beyond our comprehension. This fear can even lead to physical or emotional damage.

Diamond A diamond, in the form of a ring or otherwise, signifies the longing for perfection. Sometimes this longing is not fulfilled, resulting in a gap between expectations and reality.

Ditch A ditch, which can appear in various forms from a yawning chasm to a tiny hole, indicates primarily that the person blames others - actually everyone but himself - for the troubles that have befallen him.

Doctor A formation which indicates medical problems that can be cured.

Dog A formation in the shape of a dog suggests to the seeker that he should place more trust in his friends, and enlist their aid in solving his problems.

Doll A doll denotes feelings of guilt on the part of the seeker. The interpretation differs, depending on whether the seeker is male or female. For a woman, a doll formation indicates that she harbors guilt feelings due to unfulfilled expectations with regard to her parents. In the case of a man, the guilt feelings stem primarily from past sexual traumas. A doll is always associated with the past - never the future.

Donkey The basic explanation will always be some version of: 'Have patience. Everything will work out fine in the end!' An optimistic sign.

Door An unusual event awaits the seeker. One of the formations where more is hidden than is revealed!

Dove A very lucky sign! A dove is always a good formation... and unfortunately quite a rare one.

Dragon A dragon formation signifies an unexpected crisis that is liable to throw the seeker's life off kilter. This crisis is very difficult to avert.

Drum The seeker is full of complaints about the world in general; he blames everyone, except himself, for his troubles.

Duck A man who is hard to live with.

Dwarf A dwarf indicates that the person believes in superstitions, and is subject to the influence of illogical fears.

Eagle A change in his place of residence will have a strong impact on the seeker.

Ear Be on the alert for important news.

Ear Listen to advice and rumors. News that's on its way will lead to unexpected developments.

Earrings A formation that has meaning only if the earrings appear as a pair. It symbolizes misunderstandings in the seeker's life that are liable to have a negative impact on his relationships with others.

Earth A formation that evokes a picture of earth, in the form of a field or the like, signifies a lack of self-confidence on the part of the seeker. In the case of a woman, the formation suggests the pursuit of a man who will give her a sense of security; for a man, it signifies an inability to achieve financial security.

Egg A good sign. An egg symbolizes prosperity, success in love, a (wanted) pregnancy in the near future. A birth may be in store. New beginnings.

Elbow Always indicates problems, in two major areas: health (including sexual performance) and finances (the money problems stem from a tendency to get involved in foolish undertakings).

Elephant A formation in the shape of an elephant indicates that success will come to the seeker over time, if he stays on course, strives diligently towards his goal, and does not lose hope in the face of obstacles.

Envelope Generally, good news that will have an impact on the seeker.

Eye A protective symbol! This is a sign that "somebody up there" is guarding the seeker against the evil eye. This sign also gives him the strength to overcome obstacles.

Face A face is interpreted in the same way as the figure of a person.

Falcon The falcon, a bird of prey with a curved beak and long talons, is a good omen: the seeker's aspirations or desires will shortly be realized.

Fan An unmistakable sign of the never-ending pursuit of romantic adventure!

Faucet A significant formation. It tells us that the seeker, particularly if he is a man, is seeking help desparately. A sign of warning to a woman about to be married.

Feather The seeker's capriciousness and instability cause him to flit from job to job, from romance to romance, from one area of interest to another.

Fence Something or someone is standing between the seeker and his goals, or the realization of his ambitions.

Fern A fern signifies disloyalty on the part of the seeker or someone close to him (in the latter case, the seeker is suffering as a result).

Fire Fire, or flames, appear in different forms, and signify a high degree of sensuality on the part of the seeker.

Fish A fish is a very common formation. It is an excellent sign, indicating health, wealth and happiness to the end of time.

Fishing Rod A fishing rod, in any form, indicates that the seeker is somewhat "spaced out." His head is in the clouds, and his feet are not totally on the ground!

Fist – Threat, anger

Flag Danger threatens the seeker (or did so until recently).

Flower An unidentified flower signifies that the person's wishes and desires will be fulfilled.

Flute A tendency to withdraw into oneself and not to reveal problems; extreme shyness that is damaging to the person.

Fly A fly signifies a person who is vulnerable to self-criticism, and takes to heart everything that is said to his face or behind his back.

Fork Someone close to you is betraying you.

Fountain An excellent sign! Success, wealth and happiness in all areas of life. Boundless sexuality. Romance. A formation that is always positive.

Fox Someone close to the seeker is lying behind his back.

Frog A change, primarily work-related, lies in store for the person and will affect his life.

Fruit Fruit in any form indicates a positive direction, success, and achievement in a specific area.

Gallows A gallows indicates what lies in store for the enemies or rivals of the person seeking guidance; from his standpoint, this is a good sign.

Garden, Park A formation reminiscent of a garden or park shows that the person is seeking serenity within his close family circle.

Candle (in the field of superstitions)

The candle is a very important factor in the field of superstitions. Its main function is to bring light into places where human beings go... and to dispel the darkness, of course. Darkness is linked to the evil eye, and light to good luck. Therefore, the burning candle is a tried, tested, and accepted means of getting rid of the evil eye.

There are many superstitions linked to it. Some people light candles around a dead body (generally 12 candles) in order to create a ring of light. Others light three candles (in parallel to the Holy Trinity) for the same purpose.

The candle, especially the candle that is found in holy places - churches or the graves of saints - is important for making potions and amulets. There is a great deal of belief in the power of a "holy" candle to help a barren woman give birth, or to strengthen a man's virility... and there is no doubt that there is an inextricable link between the shape of the candle and the male member.

A burning candle gives off light, and this light is very significant. Blue light emanating from the candle always attests to good luck, for instance.

When a candle goes out during a religious ritual, it is irrefutable proof that the evil eye is in the vicinity, and that the forces of evil are invading the candle's realm!

Candles, which were made principally out of beeswax in the past, were thought to be holy because of the belief that bees originated in the Garden of Eden. This is the source of the belief that chewing the remains of holy candles fortifies the health and contributes to the curing of serious illnesses.

Candles can serve as voodoo dolls when necessary. Sticking pins in the candle while pronouncing the name of the person's sweetheart will strengthen the bond of love. The pin must be stuck in the candle, which is then lit and allowed to burn down. The scorched pins must be carried as an amulet of love.

Gate Congratulations! Something surprising and good has "hit" the seeker out of the blue!

Ghost Someone from your past is looking for you.

Giant A giant indicates feelings of inferiority.

Giraffe Impulsiveness in thought and deed leads to unexpected complications. The seeker must weigh every decision carefully.

Glass A positive sign. An object made of glass indicates that the seeker is striving with all his might to attain perfection in his actions.

Glove A significant challenge confronts, or has confronted, the seeker; now he must "take up the gauntlet."

Gondola A serious warning sign! The danger is close at hand, almost within arm's reach.

Goat A love affair that affects the seeker, despite the fact that it took place far away (physically) from where he is now.

Grandfather, Grandmother This is a formation whose interpretation is straightforward and unmistakable: the seeker's world centers around his immediate family.

Grapes Grapes in the form of a cluster signify a positive direction. The person has good reason to be happy.

Grass Grass, like a field, signifies security, stability, good family relations. A good sign.

Grasshopper Information, news or an unexpected letter will change the lifestyle and standing of the seeker.

Groom A groom always signifies... divorce! We don't know in what way the seeker will be connected with the divorce - he might be going through a divorce himself, he might be the cause of someone else's divorce, etc. - but it is clear that a divorce will affect his or her life.

Hair Anything related to hair indicates a surprise in the near future - perhaps even the fulfillment of a dream.

Hammer Hard times! Life is no bed of roses. The seeker must perform some difficult tasks.

Hand A hand always suggests a close friendship. If the fingers of the hand are spread out, the friendship is a good one; if the hand is closed into a fist, this points to a dispute between friends.

Handcuffs Disaster. Handcuffs always symbolize a bad omen, with one exception: when the handcuffs are clearly open, they signify an escape from disaster.

Handkerchief A period of mourning, which the seeker has experienced or will experience shortly.

Handle The handle of a door or window indicates a secret, a mystery, something that the seeker is trying to conceal from everyone (at times also from himself).

Hare A very important change is about to take place in the life of the seeker following news from (physically) distant individuals. The nature of the information is unknown.

Harness A horse's harness indicates a sense of inferiority on the part of the seeker.

Harp The harp, an ancient and important musical instrument, signifies harmony on the home and family fronts, and in male-female relationships. A good sign.

Hat The seeker should try to avoid making changes in his world; he'd be better off staying with things as they are, and making the most of them.

Hawk A bird identified as a hawk (or frequently, the statue of a hawk) indicates that someone is jealous of the seeker and is awaiting his downfall. Keep your eyes open!

Head The interpretation is the same as for a face or person.

Heart Love is in the offing, a new romance, a healing of a present relationship. A good sign, especially in matters pertaining to love or, even more so, marriage.

Hen A positive sign that refers to the home or family.

Hill A hill, or string of hills, signifies problems that are confronting the seeker. The size of the problems corresponds to the size of the hills.

Hoof An excellent sign. A hoof protects against the evil eye and the powers of darkness. Financial success, good health, and a guarantee that the person will triumph over problems.

Horse In principle, it is a positive figure, especially when seen to be "galloping". The hindquarters of a horse are likely to indicate that success lies beyond your reach. A figure on horseback means that the seeker has a loyal partner or companion. A horse's head indicates a daring love affair... or life in the shadow of danger!

House The shape of a house - usually in the form of a triangle on top of a square, as it appears in children's drawings - basically symbolizes happiness, stability and security.

Iceberg An iceberg or glacier always signifies great danger.

Insect This shape appears in the form of many insects, and always indicates nuisances that are numerous and troublesome, but minor; they should not be allowed to stand in the individual's way.

Island The basic interpretation is loneliness!!!.

Jail A formation containing any shape that recalls a jail, such as bars, for example, always signifies trouble. Even when the jail is "wide open," this is still a worrisome sign.

Jar A jar is interpreted as a glass object, but it can also be viewed as a cry for help from someone close to the seeker - a cry that is sometimes "disguised." This is an important formation since the person seeking help is in a serious state of distress.

Jewelry Always indicates the seeker's love of himself - more so for a man than for a woman.

Kangaroo Indicates problems involving the family. It is hard to interpret what form the solution will take or what aspect of life it will involve.

Kettle A kettle suggests minor illnesses, but also has sexual connotations (especially if the spout is visible).

Key An opportunity is opening up for you. New worlds. Take the first step and the door will open.

Kitchen A kitchen, whenever it appears, signifies a great deal of friction in the seeker's family.

Kite A significant formation. A kite symbolizes the seeker's desire to "spread his wings and fly" - to break out of his routine, try new things, broaden his horizons... and mainly to leave behind the reality in which he lives.

Knapsack A knapsack, especially a back pack, indicates indecision on the part of the seeker, or a wish to change the course of his life.

Knife Indicates that someone is separating the seeker from his spouse or lover. This situation is virtually beyond repair.

Knitting The act of knitting, as reflected by knitting needles and wool, signifies a tendency towards a stable, tranquil family life.

Ladder The seeker's efforts will bear fruit. Perseverance and diligence will always be properly rewarded.

Lake A lake tells us what awaits in the individual's spiritual realm, or points to emotional upheaval that he has undergone in the past.

Lamb A formation that points to latent sexual tendencies of the seeker.

Lamp A good sign. Financial success.

Lantern This shape is always interpreted as a desire to learn, to seek the truth, to expand one's knowledge.

Leaf Success. A sign which points in a positive direction financially.

Leaves Positive change

Legumes All types of legumes in the form of a pod (peas, ful, beans and the like) indicate financial problems. If the pod is closed, the problems will crop up in the future; if the pod is open, and the legumes themselves are visible, this is a sign that the problems are already having a negative effect.

Lemon A lemon formation indicates love.

Letter An important formation. New information that reaches you will change your life. Do not ignore it!

Lighthouse A lighthouse, which is characterized by the hint of a light at the top (in contrast to a regular tower), indicates a disaster or disappointment that has been averted.

Lily Success! The seeker is beloved by all... but he must develop some humility, and do his best to avoid getting a swelled head.

Lion The seeker has close ties with friends in high places; these contacts can be of great benefit to him.

Lizard A "mystical" formation. For the most part, it indicates a fear of the hidden, the unknown.

Lock Indicates a person who lacks financial security. Danger awaits. An open lock - the danger is imminent!

Lock of Hair A lock of hair, especially for a man, signifies that the person will receive assistance from someone close to him.

Magnet A magnet in the form of a horseshoe (with lines marked at the ends): This formation is always a sign of a good luck charm protecting the seeker.

Mailman The figure of a mailman signifies two things: the seeker is eagerly anticipating news that is likely to change his life; the seeker has doubts as to the faithfulness of his (or her) partner.

Map A road map, geographical map or atlas indicates that the person is seeking his way in life. An indistinct formation, but it indicates the direction that the interpretation will take.

Mask The seeker is concealing great pain!

Matches Many unsatisfying love affairs. A formation that is not flattering to the seeker.

Meat A formation that calls to mind meat in any form - that is, in such a way that it evokes associations with food - is indicative of the seeker's character: he is cautious, deliberate, seeks security. It would be safe to say that this is a person who sees the "flesh pots" as a goal. This formation should always be interpreted in a positive direction.

Mermaid A mermaid or siren signifies that lovers are keeping dark secrets from one another.

Mirror A formation which indicates that the person bases his actions on superstitions or emotions rather than common sense. A rare formation.

Money A formation in the shape of money or a symbol of money, such as a dollar sign ($), indicates that the person is focused on one specific aspect of life - the financial aspect.

Monster The seeker suffers from fears of unknown origin. Nightmares, insomnia, daydreams. The person fears something which he cannot define. Although this formation at times appears insignificant, it indicates a persistent and troublesome disruption in the life of the individual.

Moon A significant sign, although it is very hard to distinguish. You must be certain that it is a moon and not a banana or a ball, for example. A full moon indicates a satisfying love affair; a new moon - a love affair that has ended or an affair still in its "infancy".

Mountain A mountain, like a hill, signifies obstacles and difficulties - on a grand scale! In contrast to a hill, a mountain symbolizes an obstacle that the seeker cannot overcome by his own powers; he will need the help of others to surmount it.

Mouse A formation that denotes an act of robbery, in which the seeker was a participant or a victim.

Mouth A formation reminiscent of a mouth always indicates a fear of the "verdict" of others. Such a shape generally appears when the seeker is in the midst of a serious dispute.

Mud A mud field appears in various shapes and sizes. It indicates difficulties from which the seeker can extract himself if he makes use of his persistence and strength of will.

Mushroom Indicates a failure on the horizon in the financial sphere.

Musical Note Musical notes are always a good omen.

Necklace A necklace is judged according to a sole criterion: if it is whole, the seeker's relationship with his or her partner is stable and positive; if it is torn apart, a problem is creating distance between the partners.

Needle An important formation! It is not often seen, but when it does appear it always indicates that the seeker is a past victim of sexual abuse. What is significant is that the abuse left him traumatized to this day.

Nest A bird's nest signifies that love is the dominant factor in the seeker's life. If there are eggs (or newborns) in the nest, this love is fulfilled; if there is one or more birds sitting on the nest, the love will be satisfied in the near future. An empty nest can indicate a love that no longer exists.

Net A fisherman's net primarily signifies a broad imagination and a sense of daring in the artistic and financial spheres. A tendency to take risks.

Newspaper The formation indicates that the person is a victim of gossip, and is likewise spreading tales about others. "Do not do to others that which is hateful to you!"

Noose Beware of acting before you think, of a "hot-blooded" state that interferes with careful deliberation. Impulsive actions are liable to lead to disastrous results.

Nose A nose indicates that something has taken place without the knowledge of the seeker, or, as the expression goes, "right under his nose."

Nuts Nuts suggest "little" troubles that the individual is experiencing. Try to discern if the shells of the nuts are broken: this would indicate that the individual will overcome his troubles and problems.

Oar A cry for help! A warning sign which must not be ignored!

Octopus An octopus, taken by itself, is a bad sign. It tells the person that he must seek the help of others in solving his problems.

Olive A significant formation. Generally appears in the form of a branch, which is identifiable by the shape of the leaves and fruit. It points to serious problems in the sexual sphere; suggests troubling sexual memories.

Onion An onion shows that the person is hiding something from his or her partner that is significant enough to hurt that person. A common formation.

Ostrich An ostrich suggests journeys to faraway places, lengthy trips and a spirit of adventure.

Owl An owl is a bad sign which primarily indicates scandals and harmful gossip that will affect the seeker - and tells us that the seeker is involved in a scandal, as in "where there's smoke, there's fire."

Open hand May mean new opportunities, new relationships.

Package A common formation. A package generally indicates a surprise for the seeker in the near future. We do not know, however, exactly what kind of surprise lies in store.

Palace The figure of a palace always signifies unfulfilled ambitions. This formation is mainly seen with men.

Palm Tree A palm tree, in various forms, always indicates great respect, success and high standing achieved by the seeker.

Pants A tendency towards vanity.

Parachute Severe insecurity which impairs the person's day-to-day functioning.

Parrot A formation which signifies journeys to faraway places (it also tells us that the seeker won't run into problems there).

Peach Always a good sign! A basic shape whose interpretation is always positive. First and foremost, a peach indicates good character and romantic success; it also points to a joyous event on the horizon in the romantic sphere.

Peacock A formation that indicates hypocrisy, pretension, concealing of the truth.

Pear The pear indicates successes in the near future, or pleasant memories, especially in the areas of love and sex.

Pencil Case Indicates problems revolving around learning.

Person A formation in the shape of a person is one of the hardest signs to interpret. The figure itself can take several different forms: a man or a woman, an old person or a child. We tend to interpret male or female figures in the contexts of love, sex, marriage or divorce - in other words, male-female relationships. With regard to figures of children or old people, the interpretations focus mainly on health.

Piano The seeker has, or had, artistic and creative ambitions which have shaped and determined the course of his life.

Pig Great riches.

Pillar A pillar is generally a sign of advancement, promotion, improved status.

Pillow A formation reminiscent of a pillow always signifies the seeker's isolation.

Pine Cone A pine cone indicates that the problem lies with the seeker himself, and generally stems from medical reasons.

Pineapple A pineapple mainly says something about the seeker's personality; it signifies a person who is involved in many arguments and minor disputes, but also tends to seek reconciliation and compromise with his opponents after every quarrel.

Pipe A formation which indicates that a serious problem in the life of the seeker is about to be solved.

Pistol A significant shape. Always signifies danger to the seeker!

Pitcher A pitcher symbolizes the public standing of the seeker (in the present or future - not the past!).

Plant Success in some aspect of the arts (primarily painting).

Playing Card A card or cards indicate that the person is unstable and inconsistent in his behavior. This formation is more serious for a man than for a woman.

Pocket A formation reminiscent of a pocket points us in the direction of financial problems.

Profile The profile of a person (as opposed to a face, which is interpreted as a person) indicates that new friends will have an effect on the seeker.

Purse If you see a closed purse, the seeker should beware of his enemies. If the purse is open, it is telling the person: Believe in your own strengths! You'll find a way out of all your troubles on your own!

Pyramid A fascinating formation! The pyramid indicates an attraction to the unknown.

Rabbit A rabbit is characterized by short ears, in contrast to a hare. It indicates that the seeker must show the courage to 'stick to his guns'.

Railway Car A railway car or a trailer indicates that a loving relationship will progress to marriage.

Rainbow A rainbow symbolizes "the light at the end of the tunnel" - meaning that the seeker will ultimately find the answer to his problems. This formation is also a sign of the seeker's attraction towards mysticism.

Rake The seeker consistently ignores the little details, causing him to make a great many mistakes.

Rat The figure of a rat always indicates dangers lying in store for the seeker.

Raven Bad news. A negative sign! This formation is also tied in with mysticism and esoterica.

Rhinoceros This formation meaning is sexual incompatibility.

Rice A formation that contains rice, in the form of cooked food or scattered grains, indicates economic prosperity in the present or future.

Rifle Troubles, quarrels, arguments. Not pleasant.

Ring In general, a ring signifies marriage.

Road A road, or path, indicates that the seeker is trying to find himself in life; he is unsure of his aspirations and of his future.

Roof Financial problems for the seeker or people close to him. Note that in this formation, the roof appears only as detached from the house itself. If the roof appears as part of the house, this is a sign of stability and security.

Rose A rose tells the seeker that he should focus his attentions on the people who are close to him emotionally, especially family members. Forget material concerns for a while, and address the spiritual side of life.

Rubber Stamp A significant formation that primarily indicates a problem in the bureaucratic, official or legal sphere.

s

Salami Lack of self-confidence, excessive shyness. Problems with the opposite sex. Beware: a salami should not be viewed in any sexual context!

Salt, Salt Shaker The seeker waits for "heavenly intervention" instead of improving his situation by his own powers.

Saw Someone is undermining you, trying to come between you and someone dear to you. Don't let this happen!

Scales This formation indicates that the seeker is suffering, or feels that he is suffering, as a result of an injustice committed against him.

Scarecrow A significant formation. The figure of a scarecrow relates to the seeker's self-esteem. Pay attention to one thing: the position of the arms. If they are extended outward at the sides, it is a sign that the person possesses a high level of self-confidence and self-esteem. If no arms can be distinguished, there is a problem in the person's character.

Scissors A significant formation. Scissors signify a misunderstanding between the seeker and someone (male or female) who is very close to him. If the scissors are "open", the width of the opening indicates the degree of estrangement.

Scorpion Important! This formation warns of enemies who are plotting to bring the person down.

Sea A formation that evokes the sea always indicates that the person wishes to escape from his present life - even though he does not know what awaits him in the future. The sea signifies confusion, the search for a path in life, insecurity.

Shark An interesting formation! It always indicates that the seeker (whether male or female) fears a loss of sexual ability or reproductive capacity, as this would totally disrupt his/her life.

Sheep A good sign. A joyous event will take place shortly, or has taken place recently, primarily in the financial sphere.

Ship A shape that symbolizes good tidings.

Shirt A difficult problem is plaguing the seeker, but he refuses to discuss or share it with others.

Shoe A change for the better that has happened, is happening, or will happen in the seeker's life.

Skeleton An important formation which is encountered frequently. The position of the skeleton will help you to interpret the various areas of involvement: if you can distinguish a skull, this is a sign that danger awaits; if the skeleton is standing up, a financial crisis will shortly take place; if it is lying down, this is a sign of a very serious illness; if the skeleton is sitting, the person is not utilizing his talents.

Snail An interesting formation. A snail generally denotes a passionate, uninhibited sexual nature. A mysterious figure, most of which lies hidden.

Snake A bad sign. Someone is jealous of the seeker, hates him, and is undermining him!

Soldier It is usually treated as an ordinary figure of a "person".

Spade Danger! Stay away from past disputes and avoid future arguments.

Spear A formation that recalls a spear signifies an accident, illness or difficulty, but only on a small scale; the problem can be easily overcome, without the help of others.

Spider A spider (like a ladder) signifies that hard work will bear fruit. An additional interpretation is that the seeker has a tendency to engage in spiritual pursuits and - to a certain extent - to neglect the material aspects of life.

Spoon This formation indicates that the person will be fortunate enough to have the help of others in solving his problems.

Stair A stair or stairs indicate difficulties that the seeker is capable of overcoming, together with a spouse or lover.

Stamp A postage stamp symbolizes close ties with someone who is removed (physically) from the seeker.

Star A star shape always indicates happiness and good health.

Stone The figure of a stone of undefined shape always symbolizes a problem.

Stork A stork indicates virginity, lack of sexual experience - to the point where the seeker may even be bothered by it.

Sun A good sign! All the seeker's endeavors will be crowned with happiness, wealth and success.

Swan A very good sign. The seeker is making progress toward success, and overcoming problems that have been plaguing him.

Sword A significant formation. Always indicates a dispute between individuals who have a lot in common; for instance, a lovers' quarrel.

Table The seeker attaches a great deal of importance to social events taking place around him - whether or not he is directly involved in them.

Telephone Indicates that the seeker has a "disturbed" connection with another individual, and is in fact incapable of making decisions without the approval, explicit or implicit, of others.

Telescope The seeker is trying to find himself and his identity, and is likely to alter the entire course of his life in doing so.

Tent The figure of a tent suggests instability, troubles and even major crises. A tent is the opposite of a house, which symbolizes stability and security.

Thimble A thimble, which sometimes resembles a small wine cup, indicates changes in the life of the individual and his family.

Ticket Indicates that the seeker is destined to stake out a place for himself - be it on the home or work front - far away from his present address.

Tiger A formation that indicates a spirit of adventure, flightiness. In a man's coffee grounds, it also signifies a cruel streak, while for a woman, it points to brazen sexuality.

Tomato A difficult formation to interpret. In most cases, the tomato should be viewed in connection with sexual frustration on the part of the seeker (male or female).

Tooth, Teeth A formation which signifies that the person does things in his life that he doesn't wish to do, and pretends that everything is "okay".

Tower A tower suggests disappointment, particularly in the material realm.

Tree A good sign. The person will succeed and flourish, without losing touch with reality. Also a positive symbol for a man or woman suffering from sexual problems: a tree indicates that the solution is close at hand.

Triangle A triangle shape signifies that a good surprise is in store, in the material realm (an inheritance, a winning lottery ticket, or something in that vein).

Trumpet The seeker leans towards exhibitionism; he tends to "show off" in whatever he does.

Turtle A formation which can be identified as a turtle warns the seeker that he must keep his ears open to criticism of his actions, and listen to what others are saying in order to mend his ways.

Umbrella A great deal of anger. Continual arguments. Emotional stress as a result of unending strife. (There is no difference between an umbrella and an awning.)

Unicorn An important and widespread sign. A unicorn indicates supernatural leanings, the ability to glimpse the unknown. This formation also suggests that the seeker is influenced by supernatural powers beyond the realm of the senses.

Violin The seeker has a tendency to be arrogant and boastful. He should beware of this tendency and try to fight against it.

Volcano A volcano always says something about the character of the seeker: he or she conceals intense, passionate emotions that are likely to erupt one day and overwhelm everything in their path.

Waiter A formation which indicates that the person feels like a prisoner - someone else has the seeker "under his thumb".

Wallet A very good formation. Indicates financial gain. We can't see what's inside, but we can tell if the wallet is bulging.

Waterfall A good sign. Happiness, wealth and good health.

Weapon In general, a weapon suggests a fear that dominates the individual's life.

Whale This person thinks - or should think - "big"! His major problem is attempting to do everything on a small scale, in a limited way. This is someone who makes three separate trips to buy apples - for one apple pie! A serious problem of hesitancy and lack of self-confidence.

Wheel Success is around the corner. The seeker will be rescued from his troubles. Always a good sign.

Window Symbolizes a tendency to hide things.

Wings Wings, which always appear in pairs, indicate important news that will reach the seeker at some future point.

Witch A common formation. Always signifies "another woman" who has a significant influence on the seeker, whether male or female. It is important to understand that a witch is not necessarily an "evil woman."

Wolf A formation in the shape of a wolf indicates jealousy.

Yoke The shape of a yoke signifies a tendency on the part of the seeker to control the course of events, and to become involved in actions that lead to the willing or unwilling subjugation of others.

Zebra A formation that indicates an adventurous spirit, or an adventure in the near future - a trip to an exotic locale, a romantic fling, and so on